THE WILD COLONIAL BOYS
JACK DOOLAN AND HIS SONG

Allen Mawer has written extensively on colonial and maritime history. Major works include Ahab's Trade, a history of South Seas whaling; South by Northwest, a re-examination of the forces that have driven Antarctic exploration; Canberry Tales, a celebration of the national capital; and Incognita, on the invention and discovery of Terra Australis. Many have been short-listed for major literary awards. He has also reviewed maritime books for the *Times Literary Supplement*. His current project is a biography of Captain James Colnett RN, a Pacific pioneer trained by Cook.

THE WILD COLONIAL BOYS

JACK DOOLAN AND HIS SONG

GRANVILLE ALLEN MAWER

WITH ADDITIONAL FAMILY RESEARCH
BY JOY MUNNS

ARCADIA

First edition 2004. Revised edition 2016 by ARCADIA
the general books' imprint of
Australian Scholarly Publishing Pty Ltd
7 Lt Lothian St Nth, North Melbourne, Vic 3051
TEL: 03 9329 6963   FAX: 03 9329 5452
EMAIL: aspic@ozemail.com.au   WEB: scholarly.info

ISBN 978-1-925333-93-0

Contents

Preface

There are two Wild Colonial Boys; one is a song of infinite variety and the other is the juvenile bushranger it celebrates. For more than a century both were mysteries. The song was anonymous and the bushranger had not been identified, despite many attempts. The publication of the first edition of this book, subtitled *The Life and Legend of Jack Doolan*, revealed that there had been a bushranger who at various times was called, or called himself, John Dooling/Doolan/Dowling. Furthermore, he had been born, as the song said, in Castlemaine. The revelation was timely because the missing persons Supplement (1580–1980) to the Australian Dictionary of Biography was then in preparation. Jack was deemed worthy of inclusion but there was an important omission: I had been unable to discover what happened to the Boy after he was released from Pentridge in 1882.

That failure has now been rectified by Joy Munns, who had been told by her grandmother many years ago that the Wild Colonial Boy was her cousin. In researching the family history she found it to be true. Mary Filbin, her great-great-grandmother, was the sister of Ann Dooling nee Burke, the Boy's mother, which makes him Joy's first cousin three times removed.[1] Of itself, this indicates that at the very least the Filbin family suspected that their John Dooling, one of several living in Victoria at that time, was the Boy of the song. Had Joy's grandmother been living when my book appeared, for her it would have been no more than corroboration of family oral history. Thanks to Joy Munns the post-1882 story of the family, including the last few years of Jack Doolan's brief life, can now be told. For him and most of his siblings, the Bendigo Advertiser's forebodings about 'the strange fatality attending the children of some families' proved to be only too true.

There is no such finality about the origins of the Song, but I can report that some time before the lyrics were published it had already roamed far from Victoria. On 20 September 1879 a Queensland newspaper, the *St George Standard and Balonne Advertiser* published *An Authentic Ghost Story*. In it, a fictional drover from down south (Cargelligo in the central west of NSW is mentioned) annoys his mates by incessantly singing the song. The story names Jack Dowling as the Wild Colonial Boy – the earliest reference to Dooling/Doolan/Dowling found so far – but does not mention Castlemaine. The Boy is grouped with Ben Hall and Thunderbolt, goldrush-era bushrangers. Such oral transmission from NSW to Queensland, although here described in a work of fiction, is true to the conventions of folklore and therefore of comfort to those who would prefer the song to have folk rather than literary origins.

In spite of accumulating evidence to the contrary, some researchers still believe that the song will be found to be of Irish origin and came to Australia via America. No documentation of earlier date than the 1878–79 Australasian references in this book has yet been found in either place. The possible dates of creation range from 1872, when John Doolan of Castlemaine was convicted for bushranging, to 1881, when the names Jack Dowling and Castlemaine first appeared together in print.

Introduction

Me, yesterday I was rumour,
Today I am legend,
Tomorrow history.
   Ian Mudie, *They'll tell you about me*

According to the Oxford dictionary a legend is a traditional story believed to be true. Story becomes history only when it can be shown that the belief is based on fact. It is the historian's task to establish just how much reality there is in the legend of the Wild Colonial Boy. The task is twofold; to uncover his identify and relate it to the development of his Song.

The biographical details in the Song should be more than enough to pin him down. There are many, many versions but most agree on the main points: Jack Doolan, aka Doolin, Duggan, Dowling, Donohoe etc.[2], was born and/or reared in Castlemaine. Sometime in the 1860s, when he was fifteen or sixteen, he bailed up the Beechworth mail coach and robbed Judge Macoboy or McEvoy, adding insult to injury by giving him a lecture about injustice. Subsequently he was tracked down by troopers Kelly, Davis and Fitzroy. He wounded Kelly with his revolver but in turn was shot by Davis and captured.

The Boy might have been unable to escape the troopers but until 2004 he successfully eluded all other pursuers. The wealth

1

of detail in the Song persuaded Australia's early folklorists that the story must have an historical foundation. They wanted the details to be facts; corrupted facts if necessary, but at least something better than fictions. Their failure to find documentary evidence reinforced the story's status as legend. How could a real bushranger captured as recently as the gold rushes avoid being noticed in the newspapers, much less in prison records? Perhaps the story overlaid one from the convict era, that of Bold Jack Donohoe, who had a ballad of his own and was well-documented to boot. Russel Ward cautiously subscribed to this view.

> Many research workers have sought in vain to find an actual bushranger whose deeds could have formed the basis for the incidents recounted in the later and best-known versions of the ballad. All the evidence suggests that these 'Beechworth incidents' must be accounted for by a series of more or less fanciful alterations and additions made to the original Donahoe [sic] ballad by a series of folk singers. Between what is apparently the oldest Donahoe version and the most recent versions of The Wild Colonial Boy, there is a gradation of texts showing how the changes may have come about.[3]

So the Boy's Beechworth story was fiction after all, but then again, perhaps the researchers had been on the wrong track. The enduring popularity of Jack's Song, the basis of his status as a folk hero, lies not in his supposed history but in his philosophy. The Song is, on the face of it, a celebration of liberty rather than crime. It is by defying authority and preferring death to subjugation that Jack earns his legendary status. He embodies popular yearning to escape from social and moral restraint, to affirm the individual over the collective whatever the cost. In giving form to these abstractions he does indeed fulfill one of the functions of legend but, as we shall see, these are borrowed clothes.

The chapters that follow document the brief and inglorious life of John Doolan, juvenile bushranger. If it is not the career celebrated in the Song, that discovery cannot be any more disappointing for the reader than it was for the author. But all is not lost. In his historical, as opposed to his legendary context, the Boy provides tantalizing clues to the origin, authorship, corruption and popularization of his Song. And that process says much about Australians as we were then and as we are now. As to how a century's worth of misdirection came about, it will be shown that there is a simple explanation; it is difficult to arrive at a right answer if one starts from a wrong premise. Or, as Jack's Irish forebears might have said, if it's there you're wanting to go, sure you wouldn't be starting from here.

Sing a Song for Sixpence

If a man were permitted to make all the ballads,
he need not care who should make the laws ...
Andrew Fletcher of Saltoun

The song *Wild Colonial Boy* first came to widespread public notice during the Kelly outbreak, although the earliest documented performance was in 1878.[4] Ned Kelly appointed Sunday 27 June 1880 for his showdown with the traps but, as usual, they were late. The gang and the locals that they had detained at Glenrowan were in need of diversion. They first held outdoor games – hop, step and jump, in which Ned handicapped himself by carrying a revolver in each hand – and then, inevitably, a dance. To the strains of the concertina many a jig and a jog whiled away the afternoon and evening. Ned gallantly invited Mrs Jones, the licensee of the Glenrowan Inn, to give them a song. She begged to be excused but, anxious to please, volunteered the services of her thirteen-year-old son. She promised him sixpence if he would sing for nice Mr Kelly. Johnny Jones sang two songs and one of them was *Wild Colonial Boy*. It is not recorded whether his mother paid up; a few hours later he was dead, killed by one of the rounds the police fired blindly into the hotel. Then they burnt it down.

This footnote might have been lost to history had not Mrs Jones claimed compensation for the destruction of her hotel.

Public disquiet about police competence and integrity prompted the appointment of a Royal Commission. During its hearings questions were asked about young Jones' performance. Was Ned Kelly's name mentioned? No, testified railwayman James Reardon, 'the Kelly song' was sung by someone else.[5] Truth to tell, there was already more than one Kelly song and what the Commissioners were trying to establish was the extent to which the crowd gathered at the Glenrowan Inn might be regarded as sympathizers rather than prisoners or hostages. If the former, it might be argued that indiscriminate police fire was justified. Reardon's evidence assumed that his hearers knew the song *Wild Colonial Boy*. He quoted no lyrics and mentioned no tune because by 1881 there was no need. *Wild Colonial Boy*, even though not properly a Kelly song, was already popular enough to be in the repertoire of a 13-year-old. If Johnny Jones was guilty of anything it was of associating a bushranging ballad with Kelly, not of appropriating it by identifying him with the Boy.

Let us assume for the moment that the Commission's suspicions were not unfounded, and that many if not most of the civilians in the hotel that day were Kelly sympathizers. Reardon was adamant that the song was sung to please the gang although, as he made clear, it was not about them. The gang was being hailed as the custodian of tradition. This was a chord that resonated strongly with Ned. In the Jerilderie letter he had justified himself by reference to the discrimination and injustice that he held to be part of his Irish convict heritage. Some of the language of the letter is lifted directly from Frank the Poet's 1830s convict ballad *Moreton Bay*. While being taken to Beechworth by train for his post-Glenrowan court hearing Ned had sung some of the Kelly songs to himself. It was as though he was gathering to himself, and encouraging others to load him with, all the grievances of the colonial underclasses, aspiring to be at once their incarnation and apotheosis. In this light the siege of Glenrowan is a heroic gesture, an act of sacrificial self-immolation.

One of the conventions of tragedy is that the hero's end is foretold. Around the turn of 1878–79, some months after the Stringybark massacre but well over a year before Glenrowan, a journalist made secret arrangements to interview the Kelly gang near their bush hideout. The result was a little book published in Mansfield. The anonymous 'Authors' of *The Kelly Gang* set down the words to a number of Kelly songs. These they claimed to have taken down from dictation, and so possibly learnt them directly from the outlaws. With one named exception these songs were sung, they wrote, to 'the universal Irish street ballad tune'. They did not name it but all who read their work would have understood the reference. The tune was *Wearing of the Green*, a treason song from the Irish uprising of 1798.

The tune already had a long history by Australian standards. It had been adopted, possibly by Francis McNamara (Frank the Poet, c.1810–61), to celebrate the deeds of Bold Jack Donohoe. Donohoe was a convict bushranger who, after several years at large in the Sydney area, was killed in 1830 during a gun battle with police. In 1864 the Irish playwright Dion Boucicault featured the treason song in his play *Arrah-na-Pogue*. This hugely successful work by one of the century's more popular writers gave it a measure of respectability. Thereafter one might sing it with relative impunity, but in the delicious knowledge that it was still obnoxious to Anglo-Australian authority.[6]

The authors of *The Kelly Gang* condemned the songs they

reported. It was not distortion of facts they found offensive, but 'flippant phraseology' about serious matters. For this reason they confined themselves to quoting portions they considered harmless, and for *Wild Colonial Boy* they decided that one 'verse' would give sufficient idea of style of the whole.

> He took a pistol from his belt and waved that lovely toy.
> I'll shoot but not surrender, says the bold colonial boy.[7]

These lines are the earliest found to date that are attributed to a song entitled *Wild Colonial Boy*. Although the word 'bold' suggests Donohoe, the reference to the pistol as a toy is not found in any version of his ballads.

THE DANCE AT THE GLENROWAN INN BEFORE THE FIGHT.

Ned Kelly dances with Miss Jones, the licensee's daughter, at the Glenrowan Inn. *Australasian Sketcher*, 7 July 1880. National Library of Australia

The only record of the words allegedly sung by Johnny Jones appeared in the *Press*, a New Zealand newspaper, on New Year's Day 1881. A columnist who rejoiced in the *nom de plume* Loafer in the Street had read Melbourne reports of Ned Kelly's last stand and asked a friend if he knew the song. He was given a copy of the 'sweet idyll', from which he quoted selections at length. The words are a version of the Donohoe ballad, most evidently in the convict-flavoured chorus.

> Oh! come along my honest lad, together we will fly,
> Together we will plunder, together we will die.
> We'll gallop o'er those lofty hills, and ride across the plains,
> Until we are in slavery bound down in iron chains.

The Boy is called Jack, without surname or place of birth. He was not native-born, having 'crossed to Australia's sunny clime' (from Ireland?). He refers to his revolver as a toy. He is captured by Kelly, Davis and Fitzroy in the first printed mention of the three troopers (the real Donahoe's captors were Hodson and Mugleston). Almost contemporaneously a text that had much in common with the Loafer's was being published in Victoria.

The main departure was that it gave the Boy's name as Jack Dowling and stated that he had been born in Castlemaine, but whether the town was in Victoria or Ireland it did not say. The compiler was Arthur Thomas Hodgson. Among his publishing ventures was an irregular series of *Colonial Songsters*, words without music. The second of these, dated on the evidence of some of its other songs to 1881, gives five verses of *Wild Colonial Boy*. Hodgson's offering is the earliest printed version of the Dowling/Castlemaine song but that does not necessarily mean that its words are closest to the original. If the song is a folk ballad, as has long been thought, any of the oral versions collected and recorded since 1881 could better reflect the original, although that would be difficult to prove. If, on the other hand, Hodgson lifted the song from an unacknowledged literary source, his version is the earliest known link to that lost archetype. A third possibility is that Hodgson or a local contributor updated the Donohoe ballad and relocated the Boy from convict NSW to the Victorian goldfields. Hodgson's words are those most widely recognized today as belonging to a song with the title *Wild Colonial Boy*.

'Twas of a Wild Colonial Boy, Jack Dowling was his name,
Of poor but honest parents, was reared at Castlemaine,
He was his father's favorite, and mother's only joy
And a terror to Australia was the Wild Colonial Boy.

Eighteen hundred and sixty-one commenced his wild career,
A heart that knew no danger, no stranger for to fear
He stuck up Beechworth's mail coach and robbed judge Macoboy,
Who, trembling, gave up all his gold to the Wild Colonial Boy.

One morning, one morning, as Jack he rode along,
Listening to the mocking bird singing forth its song,
Three brave troopers they rode up, Davis, Kelly and Fitzroy,
Rode up and tried to capture the Wild Colonial Boy.

'Surrender, now Jack Dowling you see there's three to one,
Surrender in the Queen's name you outlawed plundering son.'
Jack drew a pistol from his belt and tossed the little toy,
'I'll die but ne'er surrender,' cried the Wild Colonial Boy.

He fired at trooper Kelly and brought him to the ground
When on return from Davis received an awful wound,
While thus in crimson gore he fell while firing at Fitzroy,
And that was how they captured the Wild Colonial Boy.[8]

Hogdson did not nominate a tune to which the song should be sung. In the same songster, however, he published the words to a version of *Wearing of the Green*. For sixpence, the reader got both.

It is clear that in 1881, if not before, there were two songs in circulation with the title *Wild Colonial Boy*. The one sung by Johnny Jones was essentially a Donoghoe ballad. The other celebrated a different, more modern bushranger, Dowling. There was a degree of commonality, with the Donohoe song now having elements absent from the originals but present in the Dowling song, which reciprocated by incorporating references to stealing gold that had appeared in earlier bushranging songs, including Donohoe's. There was crossover in both directions.

By the turn of the century there was nostalgic interest in what Banjo Paterson chose to call the *Old Bush Songs*. He was fearful that the oral traditions of generations of bushmen might be lost for want of setting down in print so he recruited the readers of the *Bulletin* to send in the songs they knew. He received several versions of *Wild Colonial Boy* and was able to supplement Hodgson's first two verses. Hodgson might have lacked space for them; as it was he printed the fifth verse separately, at the bottom of another page. One of Paterson's additions was similar to a verse in the Loafer's version.

> He was scarcely sixteen years of age when he left his father's home,
> And through Australia's sunny clime a bushranger did roam.
> He robbed those wealthy squatters, their stock he did destroy,
> And a terror to Australia was the wild Colonial boy.

Another expanded the Boy's interaction with Judge Macoboy.

> He bade the Judge 'Good morning,' and told him to beware,
> That he'd never rob a hearty chap that acted on the square,

And never to rob a mother of her son and only joy,
Or else you may turn outlaw, like the wild Colonial boy.

And Paterson had been sent a version of the Donohoe chorus.

Come, all my hearties, we'll roam the mountains high,
Together we will plunder, together we will die.
We'll wander over valleys, and gallop over plains,
And we'll scorn to live in slavery, bound down with iron chains.

Paterson acknowledged the anomaly of tacking a convict bolter's exhortation to the story of a goldfields tearaway, at least to the extent of noting that some of his correspondents used the same chorus for *Bold Jack Donohoe*. He cheerfully concluded that it could be made to do service for either song, and recommended both to drovers for soothing restless cattle at night. Like Hodgson, Paterson did not give a tune, but he noted the strong Irish influence in the greater number of the songs sent in and stated that 'quite a large proportion' of them were sung to *Wearing of the Green*.[9]

The strongest historical clue in the Hodgson/Paterson version is Judge Macoboy. Michael Francis Macoboy was appointed to the Victorian County Court bench in 1858. He served first at Maryborough (1858–68) and then at Bendigo. Beechworth, however, was well beyond the judicial circuit of either place. In 1950 Clive Turnbull, columnist of the Melbourne *Argus*, asked his readers, as Paterson had the *Bulletin*'s, if they could shed any light. A granddaughter of the judge, Mrs T.M. Bland, replied that her father Michael had remembered 'the incident' and told his children of it when she was young. He had also told them of the song. She thought the boy's name was Dowling but could not 'prove that point'. By now Turnbull was satisfied that there was something to the Macoboy connection. Surely, he asked, someone would be able to come up with a contemporary newspaper account. The silence was profound.[10] A few years later Frank Hardy interviewed two other Macoboy descendants. They were most likely the daughters of the judge's third son, James. They told him that a song about the incident had become current in their father's lifetime and that their brother had whistled the tune to tease him.[11] They did not state that the song was true, which presumably they would have had they known. James Macoboy's annoyance might have been no more than the resentment of a respectable *paterfamilias* that his long-dead father continued to be the butt of a vulgar song. Of the two family recollections that recorded by Hardy is the more credible.[12]

At that time folklorist John Meredith was collecting oral and printed versions of the Donohoe song. One had been unearthed in the 1890s by M.H. Ellis, who had it from an ex-convict named Timms. In the Timms version Donohoe is named as the Wild Colonial Boy. The verses tell Donahoe's story and the chorus has him 'cross the wild Blue Mountains, and scour the Bathurst plains'. Meredith, like Ellis, accepted this as evidence that the chorus went back to convict times. The Wild Colonial Boy Dowling must be Donohoe under an alias. They did, after all, share the same nickname and initials. And if this was just circumstantial, would another candidate please step forward? It was a good point. In spite of the biographical and geographical detail in the Boy's song, no-one had been able to find a bushranger named Dowling, or Doolan, or Duggan, or any of the other variants of his name. Meredith and Ellis preferred to believe that the Boy was a real, misnamed bushranger rather than a fiction, even if most versions of the Song other than Timms' mentioned facts far removed in time and place from Donohoe and described exploits that bore no relation to Donohoe's own. Because Donohoe had been born in Dublin, as many versions of his ballads relate, and died in New South Wales, Meredith had to dismiss Castlemaine as 'ballad cliche' and Macoboy and Beechworth as corruptions. In spite of its weaknesses his interpretation was widely accepted.[13]

Ironically, Meredith was undoing that which he was most keen to preserve. Recall that a legend is a traditional story believed to be true. If the story can be brought into the province of history, fact replaces faith. By identifying the Wild Colonial Boy with Donohoe Meredith was denying the legend. There was, however, one who kept the faith. John Manifold was also a folklorist, but when it came to the provenance of songs like *Wild Colonial Boy* he was as much interested in process as in product. He was reasonably sure that there was a Jack Doolan of Castlemaine, even though he could not be found, but that was beside the point. If the song was largely a fiction, so much the better. The important thing was that an individual or a group of Australians, sometime, somewhere, had expressed in song something of their values and aspirations. Those sentiments must have struck the same chord in those that passed the song from voice to voice or it would not have survived to be collected. *Wild Colonial Boy* is a song of freedom and defiance of authority. It expresses a passion for justice and celebrates courage in the face of odds. It is not so much the vehicle that matters, but the moral baggage it carries.[14]

When, years later, the Hodgson songster came to light in the Mitchell Library it undid the main connection that Paterson and Meredith had made to Bold Jack Donohoe. As printed by

Hodgson, *Wild Colonial Boy* had no chorus. Instead, the last line of each verse was reprised. This was a separate song that had become blended with the Donohoe ballad by the time Paterson collected it. Doolan had not stolen Donohoe's clothes; someone had planted them on him. In the fifth edition of his monumental *Australian Folk Songs* (1994), Ron Edwards noted that Hodgson had published his songster in the supposed home town of the Boy. Was this significant? Perhaps. Castlemaine is only forty kilometres from Bendigo and Maryborough. Its court was earmarked for Macoboy until some of the inhabitants successfully lobbied for a local man.[15] Was it possible that the Wild Colonial Boy, instead of bailing up the judge, had appeared before him? Macoboy's main jurisdictions were civil but four times a year he chaired the General Sessions that heard less serious criminal matters.

In 1980 Pat Edwards interpreted the story of the song for children, admirably summing up the state of knowledge about the Boy after a century of inquiry.

> No one knows who Jack Doolan was – or even if he lived at all. Some people believe the song is really about Jack Donahoe [*sic*], the famous outlaw of the 1820s but that the name was changed because it was forbidden for convicts to sing of bushrangers and outlaws. Jack Donahoe was shot and killed long before 1861, so perhaps there was a boy once who longed to be a famous bushranger – just as we've imagined.[16]

That was Manifold's point. The Boy is our generic outlaw. His values are what we, collectively over time, have made them. Manifold assumed that if he had been able to find Doolan, the Boy's exploits would reflect the values in the song. Why otherwise would he become a subject for the balladeers? It was, as we shall see, a false assumption. What follows is the story not only of Jack Doolan but of his transformation from what he was into what we, as Australians, wanted him to be.

Castlemaine, the Boy's birthplace. S.T. Gill, Market Square, Castlemaine, Forest Creek, c.1857. National Library of Australia

The Boy Who Stabbed John Zahner

'Tis of a wild colonial boy, Jack Doolan was his name

John Doolan was born on 28 April 1856 at Castlemaine in the Victorian goldfields, the second son of William Dooling and Ann Burke. How he came to be known by a surname different to his father's will become apparent hereafter. The Doolings did not trouble to register the birth in spite of the fine for which they would have been liable had their omission become known. They made an entry in the family bible and left it at that.

His father and his mother were ex-convicts, transported to Tasmania in 1848 and 1849 respectively.[17] They had each been sentenced to seven years, he for robbing a dwelling house in Tipperary, she (with her sister Mary Filbin) for burglary in Wexford.[18] In 1852 these penal escapees from the Great Potato Famine were given permission to marry.[19] Their first two children, William (1852) and Catherine (1853) were born in Hobart.[20] It was probably at the expiration of William senior's sentence in May 1854 that the family crossed Bass Strait and began chasing dreams of gold from rush to rush across central Victoria. After John there was Thomas (1859) and Patrick (1861), both born at Miner's Rest near Ballarat. James (1863) was born in Ballarat itself. John apart, all these births were registered.[21] The last child, Annie, was born at Bendigo in 1866 and like John she was not registered.

William senior was not a successful digger. A growing family made him less mobile than the single men. Vandemonians, as the Tasmanian ex-convicts were known (with the emphasis on demon), were almost as suspect as the Chinese when it came to goldfields crime and even a family man might be suspect if neighbours knew his history. Sometime between 1863 and 1866 the Doolings and their in-laws the Filbins had moved to Bendigo. The Doolings opened a sly-grog shanty in Barnard Street.[22] Bendigo, officially Sandhurst, was by then the great hope of the goldfields. The easily-won alluvial deposits had been largely worked out. The future lay in deep quartz mining. It was expensive, difficult and dangerous but if it could be made to pay anywhere that place was Bendigo, where great reefs of the stuff ran under the town. The promise of riches yet to come was what maintained Bendigo's size and status as the second or third city of Victoria. A more or less steady population of about 26,000, including the adjacent town of Eaglehawk, provided better job opportunities than elsewhere as other goldfields towns mushroomed and then just as quickly fell into decline or extinction.

For Jack, as we might presume to call him, the still-raw community of Bendigo would have been the first in which he experienced anything like domestic stability. He got some basic education but it was of little interest to him. His activities as a street arab brought him to the attention of municipal officers and local magistrates. With his brothers he became known for petty mischief like using a shanghai and damaging plants in the Camp Reserve. When he turned twelve, in 1868, his father upped his age a year and apprenticed him to Joseph Abbott, one of Bendigo's leading citizens, at the New Times boot factory and store in Pall Mall. The premium payable to the boy's master would have been a major commitment of Dooling funds; Jack was an investment in the family's future. For half a year the boy stuck to his last. It was his misfortune, however, to be working alongside John Zahner.

Zahner was three years older than Jack, and they did not get on. The older boy was a tormenter if not a bully. Jack was probably not his only victim, but he seems to have taken it more to heart than others. In particular, he took offence at the suggestion that he had stolen some cherries. Matters came to a head on Friday 8 January 1869. The two were at work. Jack was scraping the bottom of a boot with a broken knife. Zahner claimed that it was one he had lost a week earlier and demanded the loan of Jack's in return. Insults may have passed. Jack refused on the grounds that Zahner would make his knife blunt. Zahner took the broken knife from him and returned to his bench. Jack responded as a twelve-year-old would; he made faces. Zahner told him to be quiet, came over and gave him a shove. Jack took out his clasp knife, opened it, and ran at the older boy. They scuffled and then went back to work. Half an hour later Zahner claimed that he had been stabbed. John Morgan, another employee, pulled off the stout leather apron the boy was wearing and found blood to be flowing from under his shirt. There was not much blood, but someone ran off to fetch Mr Abbott.

Abbott demanded an explanation of his wayward apprentice.

Jack said that it would have served Zahner right if he had killed him – he would not be called a thief by anyone. 'It would be worse to be called a murderer', his employer replied, and dismissed him on the spot. Dr Betham was called. He found that the abdominal wall had been penetrated but the wound was not serious. Everyone went home and there, it seemed, the matter rested.

Not for long. On the following morning Zahner's father Charles made a complaint at the police station. He had an unsavoury reputation but his rights under the law were the same as any man's: Detective Alexander was sent to Barnard Street to arrest 'John Doolan' for inflicting serious bodily injury. And it was as John Doolan he was known for the next two years, except when he adopted an alias or the authorities confused him with one of his brothers, which did happen, as we shall see. The Boy was carried away to the lockup and appeared before the Police Court four days later. He was not about to be railroaded. He had retained a solicitor and his mother had engaged barrister James Martley on his behalf. On the bench were Police Magistrate Lachlan McLachlan, otherwise 'Bendigo Mac', the terror of disorderly persons since the early days of the rush, and John McIntyre, a former mayor. John Zahner took the stand. He was fit enough to tell his side of the story but before he could be cross-examined he appeared to become 'very weak and faint'. Dr Betham intervened to say that Zahner had been spitting up blood that morning and was not fit to give evidence. He should be in hospital. The case was remanded until it was clear that Zahner was out of danger.[23] Martley sought bail for his client, a 'mite of a boy' who he said was unlikely to go missing before the hearing resumed. McIntyre was unimpressed:

> He may be a mite of a boy but he is a great scamp. He
> has been frequently before me. The bench will take two
> sureties of £50 each.

Martley protested: 'Why, your worship, that is two pounds in
money for every pound weight of the boy's body!' McIntyre was
unmoved:

> That may be, but his body is heavy enough to throw
> himself upon others and injure them in a manner to
> endanger their lives.[24]

Sureties in such amounts were of course beyond the resources of
the family; Jack remained in custody. The case did not resume
until 19 January. By then McLachlan had gone on leave and the
magistrates' bench was occupied by a mixed bag of local Justices
of the Peace, some of whom begrudged the obligations that went
with the title. Zahner resumed his evidence, but this time he had
to face cross-examination by James Martley. Martley was a large
figure on a small stage: a decade earlier he had been Solicitor-
General in the Nicholson Government, now he was the lion of
the Bendigo Bar.

Martley began by gently reminding Zahner that there had
been others present during the alleged incident. He then asked
Zahner whether he had called Jack a thief and an Irish pig.
Zahner fell into the trap. He had not, he said, and if Morgan or
Railton, the others present, swore he did they swore lies. He also
had not called the prisoner a loafer. Morgan and Railton were, of
course, promptly called and enough was extracted from them to
establish that either on the day in question or earlier Zahner had

called Jack a thief and/or Irish loafer. As there was no denying the wound Martley was arguing mitigation, and he had a case. Had not Betham testified that the wound was not serious? And age was relevant: Abbott testified that he had been told that Jack was thirteen when apprenticed in May 1868; Martley produced the family bible which showed that he would not turn thirteen until 28 April next.

The magistrates had wide discretion. Jack's case could have been dealt with by them as an assault had they wished. Bendigo Mac might well have done so, but summary justice was not for the reluctant amateurs on the bench that day. After the prosecution had closed its case Martley addressed them, with some exasperation. He could see from their faces, he said, that they had made up their minds to commit the boy for trial; in his view, a good whipping would serve better. If the case was to go to a jury, could there at least be moderate bail? Certainly, said the bench, in two sureties of £25 each and Jack's father in the sum of £50. It might as well have been £500. At the rising of the court William was still unable to post bail. Jack was committed to the next sitting of the Circuit Court. In spite of Betham's evidence to the contrary the charge was grievous bodily harm.[25]

Jack was doubly disadvantaged. To avoid dealing with the matter themselves the magistrates had inflated the charge. Had they done their duty Jack would have had right of appeal to the local circuit of General Sessions, where newly-arrived Judge Michael Macoboy was already demonstrating a disposition to be lenient with under-age offenders. Instead, this twelve-year-old's case would be heard by no less a personage than the Chief Justice of Victoria. Sir William Stawell was noted for many things, but leniency was not foremost among them. On the other hand, given Jack's intemperate remark about it being no harm if Zahner were dead, the charge could have been attempted murder, a hanging offence.

The Circuit Court convened in Bendigo on 13 February, an unlucky day for Jack. He pleaded not guilty and a jury was empanelled but the prosecutor merely had to go over the evidence given in Police Court. The jury found Jack guilty but recommended mercy on account of his age. Stawell was disposed to agree but first he waved the judicial finger at Jack, warning him that 'giving way to passion' might one day see him placed at the bar charged with a capital offence. He sentenced Jack to twelve months' imprisonment, which would begin with a fortnight's sample of life under the broad arrow in Sandhurst Gaol but be followed by a year in the reformatory 'that he might escape contamination from other prisoners'.

Reformatory

Of poor but honest parents he was born in Castlemaine

When Jack fell into the clutches of the penal system in February 1869 he and his family came under a degree of official scrutiny unknown since the parents had left Tasmania. The reformatory admission sheet recorded that his parents were living 'in poor circumstances'. Jack himself could both read and write, but only indifferently. He was of the Roman Catholic persuasion and had been born in Castlemaine.[26] The admission sheet gave no source for this last piece of information but the date of birth also recorded is the one that Martley had cited from the family bible. It is reasonable to conclude that both facts came from the same source.

Offenders under the age of fifteen were designated criminal children and sent to the reformatory. In Jack's day that meant assignment to the brig *Sir Harry Smith*, permanently moored in Hobson's Bay at the mouth of the Yarra. She was a fully masted and sparred vessel on which boys could be trained to become seamen, or at least learn the rudiments of sailmaking and ship's carpentry. Jack was again put to shoemaking, the only boy of that trade aboard in 1869. As a result, the quantum of his year's work is precisely recorded in the inspector's annual report: Jack made 94 pairs of boy's boots. His labour was costed at 5/6 the pair and so was worth £25/17/- in total. The inspector also reported that while reformatory discipline had been poor at the beginning of 1869 it had improved during the year.[27] Jack's conduct was good and he went back to Bendigo with a clean sheet. He was released to the custody of his father, but this appears to have been an end to paternal responsibility. William senior is conspicuous by his absence from his son's subsequent misadventures.

Jack's return to his home was not hailed by the appearance of a comet but there was a small sign that by the standards of a more perfect world he had been unjustly treated. Charles Zahner appeared in the Bendigo police court charged with indecent exposure. The keeper of the Camp Reserve said that Zahner had

The reformatory ship in Hobson's Bay. G.G. McCrae, Sir Harry Smith (trainer), W[illia]mstown Lt. Handfield, c.1865. National Library of Australia

24

wilfully exposed his person 'amongst the willows' in the company of Mary Ann O'Neil. He had been cautioned for a similar offence eight months previously, and the police now stated that he was a reputed loafer and associate of prostitutes. That was good enough for Bendigo Mac. Zahner got twelve months, as did the unfortunate Mary Ann, who was guilty of nothing more than plying her trade.[28] This happened, *mirabile dictu*, on the very day that Jack's sentence expired.

Although Jack had been well behaved on the training ship, the reformatory inspector could not say the same for some of his fellow inmates. Absconding was easy for anyone who could swim moderately well or steal the boat used for training. The Sandridge police were often called upon to round up bewildered boys who, having made it ashore, were still all at sea in an unfamiliar locality, but some made it to freedom and among those was Edward James Donnelly. Ned, like Jack, was a goldfields boy, born in Inglewood. His father Martin was long dead and his mother Catherine, nee Hallinan, had remarried, so Ned was officially the stepson of Denis Healey and was sometimes called by that surname.[29] He was a year older than Jack and a year ahead of him in crime. In May 1868 John Hannon, shoemaker, had made the mistake of asking him to mind a horse for a minute or two. That was near Axedale, 25 kilometres east of Bendigo. It was the equivalent of giving a modern thirteen-year-old the keys to a sports car and telling him on no account to drive it. Ned went joyriding, and was supposed to have been on his way to Echuca when intercepted a fortnight later near Huntly. Vexed, he said that had he known he was being followed he would have ridden the horse into the Campaspe River, presumably to cover his tracks. The most that his defence could do for him was to thank Hannon for not pursuing a charge of horse stealing. The lawyer added, unprompted, that the best thing for the boy would be reformatory. Bendigo Mac agreed. Ned would do a week in goal for theft of saddle and bridle and five years in the reformatory to keep him out of mischief.[30] When Jack arrived at the training ship nine months later the two struck up a friendship. Such relationships between older and younger boys gave rise to allegations that the reformatory was a school of crime, but they were also of concern to the authorities for another reason.

> ... when boys attain a certain age there is a tendency to abominable practices amongst them, and you cannot keep a watch upon that so well on board a ship.[31]

Three weeks after Jack's release, and with three years of his own sentence yet to serve, Ned absconded.[32] Wearing ship's uniform, which consisted of a blue serge jumper with matching trousers and bare sailors' feet, he should have been easily identified and picked up, as were the two boys he escaped with. That he was not may in part be attributable to the creative use of an alias. He did not choose just any name, but that of another Bendigonian on the training ship. In 1868 he and William Jones had been sentenced only a week apart and had been together in Sandhurst Gaol. They were of the same age and sufficiently similar in build and appearance to confuse any policemen reliant on written description alone. They had been registered in the reformatory records with sequential numbers. What was even better, Jones absconded a month after Donnelly and for a brief period both were at large.[33] When Jones was recaptured the search for him ceased and a William Jones could be abroad with an impunity that Edward James Donnelly, wanted, could not. For twenty months Ned eluded capture and by late 1871, if not earlier, he was back on his home turf. There he looked up Jack Doolan. Jack had kept his head down. He had not transgressed again, or if so it had not come to the attention of the law. There was however the curious episode of the Beehive fire.

Saturday Night at Sandhurst, the Bank window. R. Bruce, c.1873. National Library of Australia

The Beehive was the largest and most celebrated emporium in Bendigo. More importantly, the verandah that graced its Pall Mall frontage was the scene of Bendigo's most feverish stock exchange and its upstairs rooms housed the registered offices of a large number of sharebrokers and mining companies. If Bendigo had a business hub the Beehive was it, and in 1871 the town was in the throes of a gold rush scarcely less manic than that of '51. The scramble now was not for physical gold but for scrip in mining companies. There were fortunes to be made by joining the Great Extended Hustlers or participating in the Golden Fleece. Of a Saturday evening, as the burghers of Bendigo promenaded down Pall Mall, their pockets lined with paper promises of riches to come, past banks in whose illuminated windows gleamed the golden spoil of the week's crush, it must have seemed to a poor boy that the entire world was wealthy save him and his.

Be that as it may, around dawn on 25 August 1871 one Harward, an early-rising sharebroker with offices in the Beehive Chambers, saw flames reflected in the windows. He ran into the street for help and sent a passing youth to ring the fire bell in the Camp Reserve, a hundred metres or so away. Vital minutes passed but no bell was heard. Then the youth, whose name Harward later recalled was Doolan, returned to say that he had been unable to get into the bell tower. By the time others had effected entry and rung the bell to summon the brigade the fire was beyond control. In an hour the whole building was consumed. Strenuous efforts had been made to save records and goods ahead of the flames but, as daylight strengthened, the throng of spectators could see scraps of charred scrip fluttering down to litter the streets. The excitement usually attending a spectacular fire was

Fire at Beehive Store. Sandhurst

Fire at the Beehive Store. O.R. Campbell, 1871. National Library of Australia

absent. Even those not watching their own securities, unbanked cheques and records go up in smoke understood that the fire could be a death blow to investor confidence and therefore to the town's prosperity. First estimates put the total loss at £100,000. The *Bendigo Evening News* was suspicious.

> ... it appears almost certain and beyond dispute, that if the fire had originated in any accident or from incautious use of fire overnight, that the premises would have been burnt to the ground before 6 o'clock this morning or, at all events, that fire or smoke would have been seen before midnight or some time during the night. [On the other hand, a] fire may be simultaneously ignited in var-

ious places so as to produce a conflagration, such as occurred this morning, with little or no warning ... Again, it is scarcely conceivable how a fire accidentally arising ... would have simultaneously burst, as it did, through the whole roof of the building: one end or centre part of the building would have been first consumed. As to the motives which could have influenced an incendiary – that is a matter for the police ... The motives that lead to human conduct are so various as to be sometimes quite inscrutable to human apprehension.[34]

There should have been a coronial inquest but no report of it appears in the Bendigo papers.[35] The identity of the youth Doolan remains a mystery, but a coroner might have been interested in what the youngster had been doing abroad at that hour. One legitimate excuse was newspaper delivery and the *Independent* reported that one of its runners, who it did not name, had come into the office at 6.10 am with news of the fire and had then been sent to ring the fire bell.[36] Was it Jack? His parents' home in Barnard Street was only half a kilometre away across the Camp Reserve. The two of his brothers still at home were ten and seven years old, too young to be referred to as youths rather than boys, much less old enough to be deliberate incendiaries. The Beehive could not be seen from the Dooling house so it is unlikely that the failed bell-ringer, if a member of the family, had been attracted to the fire by the commotion. It had scarcely started by the time he appeared. All that can be said with certainty is that there were other serious fires in business premises in the centre of Bendigo over the next few months and, though fire was unremarkable in a largely timber town, these had enough in common to raise the spectre of arson.

Macoboy's Law

He stuck up Beechworth's mail coach and robbed judge Macoboy.

It is doubtful that in 1871 Jack was aware that since his stint in the reformatory he had come into at least part of a man's estate. Although still years short of his majority he had passed his fifteenth birthday and so in criminal liability, but not in legal rights, he was an adult. Should he again offend there would be no concessions on account of his youth. Indeed, youth itself was almost an offence in the eyes of some, not least the *Bendigo Evening News*, which pontificated at length on 'The Origin of Larrikinism and the Means of Suppressing It'.

> The metropolitan and provincial Press, for months past has teemed with accounts of more or less disgraceful outrages committed by the boys and hobbydahoys who are now designated – 'larrikins'… it is high time some stringent steps were taken to bring into operation to repress such precocious tendencies that will otherwise grow with the growth of the perpetrators until the latter become matured ruffians or criminals…Since larrikins have been deprived of the needful discipline of the school of Good Mothers the only remedy is for it to commence with the birch, and resort to flogging.[37]

Politicians were acutely aware that such sentiments were widespread. Larrikinism was on the rise, especially in Melbourne, and there had been sustained pressure on the government to act.

Its response was to commission a review of the effectiveness of prison both as a deterrent to crime and as a place where criminals might be reformed. In August 1870 it appointed Chief Justice Stawell, the judge who had tried Jack Doolan, to chair a Royal Commission into penal and prison discipline.

Among the witnesses was Macoboy, the judge who had not tried Jack Doolan. He offered no evidence about being robbed on the Beechworth mail, although like everyone else he knew that Harry Power had bailed it up before his recent capture. The tale he did tell was of two boys he described as 'little bushrangers', who had appeared before him at Echuca General Sessions. One was sixteen, the other was fourteen and they were guilty of a number of cases of horse stealing. Macoboy felt that the older boy had led the younger astray but even so would have sent both to the reformatory if it had been up to him. As the law stood he had no option other than to send the sixteen-year-old to prison: 'My intention was to keep him from harm; but he was obliged to be sent to gaol, being over fourteen'. So fearful was Macoboy of what happened to youngsters in gaol that he favoured corporal punishment, which was already allowed but only in addition to a term of imprisonment. Macoboy wanted it available as a substitute: 'They might get a gentle whipping. I think such a birching as a schoolmaster would give on the breech; I think that is the better way'. The Commissioners pricked up their ears: 'Flog them, and fine the parents if they did not look after them?' Macoboy gently replied that by whipping he meant just that. To be whipped like a schoolboy was a painful embarrassment; to be flogged with the cat of nine tails was degrading. Brutal punishment legitimised brutality. Punishment should endeavour to improve.

Michael Macoboy was speaking with the authority of one who for thirteen years had chaired General Sessions of the Peace in circuit towns throughout central Victoria, based first at Maryborough and then at Bendigo. He had come to Australia early in the gold rushes with a reputation earned at the Irish and English Bars. Unusually for a County Court judge he had chosen to live in the communities he served rather than commute on circuit from Melbourne.[38] Although his health was poor and there were rumours from time to time that he would soon retire to Europe, these were always strenuously denied. His views were in many respects at odds with those of hard-liners like Sir Redmond Barry. He looked on punishment more as a means of protecting society against recurrence of the offence than retribution against the individual. He recalled that while he was chairing the General Sessions at Avoca cattle stealing was rife. To deter it he passed one sentence of eight years. It effectively stamped out the epidemic. That achieved, he might give only six months for a similar offence.

He had strong views about long sentences. Life, thirty, twenty, even sixteen years were too much. They extinguished hope. The maximum, given the continuance of capital punishment for 'atrocious crimes', should be ten years. Macoboy also observed that he had never given a cumulative sentence in his life.

> I have noticed that persons have been astonished why I have not given it. I apply the one test. I say, it is perfectly unavailing to try a man on three or four cases; and I give for the first offence what I consider an adequate sentence for the preservation of society; and if I had to try him over again, I should only give the same sentence.[39]

Macoboy was not alone in his views about juvenile offenders but his experience lent them considerable weight. When the Royal Commission reported in May 1871 it recommended prevention rather than repression.

> Juvenile crime is mainly the offspring of ignorance, first in the parents, and then in the children; in a lesser degree it arises from habitual idleness, from the circumstances of a new country, which are adverse to the sentiments of reverence and obedience in the minds of the young, and from the culpable neglect of parents to look after the moral training of their children and to exercise over them proper control.

Children should be kept at home, away from those 'vicious associations' that contaminated morals and depraved manners. An efficient system of public education was nothing less than an 'imperious necessity'. Immoral and indecent public entertainments should be suppressed and 'healthful and rational recreation' substituted with the encouragement of the Government. And if, in spite of the wholesome influence of lyceum and gymnasium, some of the young continued to offend? Incarceration of youths, they said, either together or with adults, was a 'palpable and serious' evil; young persons invariably sank morally to the level of the worst amongst whom they were confined. The only available substitute was 'personal chastisement'.

> It cannot be denied, however, that there exists, and properly, a strong repugnance to the infliction of corporal punishment on youths as a sentence. The objections taken to it are, that it is calculated to destroy self-respect and permanently degrade the moral feelings; and that, when once established as a legal penal-

> ty, there is a disposition to apply it too frequently and indiscriminately. There is certainly great force in these objections; but nevertheless they yield, in our opinion, to the absolute necessity of adopting corporal punishment as the only alternative for imprisonment. It is the lesser of two evils.

To prevent abuse, the Commission recommended that at least two justices be present when sentence was passed, one of whom should be the police magistrate, that a special report should be made in each case, that 24 hours' solitary confinement on bread and water in the lock-up (not gaol) could be substituted or added, and that the power be limited to police districts so authorized by the Government for a definite period. And the chastisement was to be inflicted with birch rod only (not the lash) to a maximum of 'five-and-twenty stripes', all to be given at the one time.[40]

To modern sensibilities it may seem odd that concern for convicted children should lead to a proposal for corporal punishment, but in the 1870s a dozen stripes of a master's birch was not regarded as excessive even for something as trivial as misbehaviour at school.

Judge Michael Francis Macoboy

The Sugarplum Kids

Jack drew a pistol from his belt and tossed the little toy.

At Huntly, on the evening of 16 December 1871, Ned Donnelly broke through a window into the hut of Patrick Hehir, labourer, and stole a suit of his clothes and two shirts. Huntly is a few kilometres north of Bendigo. Ned's mother resided at White Hills, along the road between the two. Why Ned was in need of such items remained obscure until the end of the month. Then he and Jack took to the road. For the Doolan family, it was the beginning of a tragic summer.

What followed reads like nothing so much as a conscious program of kitting out for the bushranging life.[41] The first requirement, obviously, was a horse. Ned knew where they could get one (he seems to have been quite keen on horses). John Steer, wheelwright and blacksmith, had turned his chestnut out on Axedale Common. The last he saw of it was on Boxing Day.

Bridget Foley, a widow, lived alone and isolated on a smallholding near Axe Creek. Her nearest neighbour was about a quarter of a mile distant. At nine o'clock on New Year's Eve she was about to go to bed when there was a knock on the door. 'What do you want?' she asked. 'Bread', was the answer, 'and if you do not open the door we will break in or come down your chimney'. Reluctantly she opened the door and saw a revolver being pointed at her by two boys, neither of whom she knew.

Ned and Jack demanded what money she had and threatened her life. She found 3/6 in her pocket and gave it to them. For half an hour she watched as they unsuccessfully ransacked the house for more, Ned swearing the while and threatening the widow with criminal assault. They took two billycans, a canister of tea and some fowls before melting into the night. Terrified for her life Bridget Foley did not report the crime, telling only Samuel O'Brien, a passer-by, later that night.

In the days that followed the boys committed a number of petty thefts to provision themselves. They went to a slaughter yard to lift some beef and mutton. From a farmyard they obtained honey and other delicacies. Now while one horse might carry two boys bareback without much difficulty, there was a growing problem with the impedimenta they were accumulating. Another horse would have been useful, but perhaps Jack could not ride. In any event, they opted for a cart. Ned also knew where there was one of those. Nine days after the raid on widow Foley, Patrick O'Donaghue was woken between four and five o'clock in the morning by the sound of voices coming from the harness room that adjoined the stable on Patrick Hallinan's farm, six kilometres north of Axedale. 'Who is that', he called out, 'is that Patsy Ryan?' 'Yes', said the face that appeared at the bedroom window. O'Donaghue could see that it was not, and asked the face what it wanted. 'The harness for the spring cart.' 'Ask himself (i.e. Hallinan)', O'Donaghue suggested. The face, which was Ned's, demanded that the harness be handed out. O'Donaghue moved to the door and asked 'what the hell do you want?' 'Blow out his brains!' said another voice: that was Jack's contribution. O'Donaghue called loudly for his master: 'Paddy!', which prompted Ned to force the door and present the revolver at him.

John Doolan, 15, bushranger. PROV, VPRS 515, Central Prisoner Records Males, Unit 14, No. 9556. Keeper of Public Records, Public Records Office, Victoria

'Another word or your life'. Ned took the harness from the wall and covered O'Donaghue while Jack placed Steer's horse in the shafts of Hallinan's cart. For good measure they also took a saddle and bridle before taking to the Campaspe road, headed north.

From his bedroom in the main house Hallinan heard the cart pass. O'Donaghue was hammering at his door before the robbers were even out of sight. The boys had been dressed in men's clothes and O'Donaghue reported them as men, armed men. Hallinan immediately saddled up and went full gallop in pursuit. As it was now daylight he soon caught sight of the cart but the effort had exhausted his horse. He stopped at Adelaide Vale station to borrow another and, freshly mounted, continued to shadow the cart, riding through the bush rather than along the road. With O'Donaghue's warning in mind he made sure that he remained out of sight.

Near Adelaide Vale the road forked and the boys took the Sandy Creek road, away from the river and towards Huntly. Ned was a creature of habit. He was following the same route that he had taken four years earlier when he stole Hannon's horse. It must have seemed to the boys that life was good. Their one horsepower, two-wheeled, steel-sprung vehicle was the nineteenth century's equivalent of the Holden utility; a working vehicle true, but one that could be driven with style and even a certain flashness. They had 3/6 and a revolver in their pockets, men's clothing, food, cooking utensils, and a saddle and bridle for the horse. Their bushranging outfit was complete.

Their plan, whatever it was, went awry when they were still six kilometres from Huntly. The road had left the bush and was now traversing more open country. The boys could see that there was someone behind them. Were they being followed? Was it the police? They came to a crossroad: on to Huntly and Echuca or left to White Hills and Bendigo? It was a time for cool heads and stout hearts but the boys had neither; they headed for home and mother. A few minutes later Hallinan reined in at the intersection and weighed up the situation. He could follow the cart into Bendigo but Huntly was closer. He spurred his horse across country to the Huntly police station.

It was six o'clock and Constable William Davidson was hardly astir, but in a matter of minutes he was mounted and in hot pursuit down the Bendigo road, with Hallinan trailing behind on his second spent horse before breakfast. Davidson was a Crimean War veteran. Even though he had armed himself with two double-barreled revolvers[42], it is to his great credit that he was prepared to ride off alone after what had been reported to him as two armed bushrangers. At the Epsom railway gate he was told that the cart had just passed through. When at a quarter to seven he reached White Hills and could see the cart ahead of him he spurred to overtake. The boys must have seen him coming. They whipped their horse up to a furious pace but it was not sustainable. Already Steer's chestnut had pulled the cart some thirty kilometres, and that in a little over two hours. Davidson bailed them up opposite the Robin Hood Hotel. It was a nice touch.

He was expecting to arrest two armed men. He found two frightened boys who did not attempt to resist but quietly allowed themselves to be handcuffed. In Jack's pocket Davidson found a percussion revolver. It was loaded and capped, ready for use. He asked for their names. 'William Jones', said Ned. 'James Kelly', said Jack. Hallinan, who had managed to catch up, said nothing but identified his cart. It was a sad little convoy that trailed into Bendigo. To one observer

> They seemed very much frightened at the sudden and unexpected manner in which their glorious career was brought to a close, and perhaps the fear of what was to come made them more uncomfortable than the reflection of what they had lost.[43]

The boys were lodged in the watch house. Later that morning they were taken before the Mayor at police court. Their aliases were exposed by the police, who recalled the boys from their training ship sentences. Or partly exposed; Jack was confused with his youngest brother because he had called himself James. The *Bendigo Advertiser* described Jack as of an 'unfortunate family', instancing 'his elder brother convicted of stabbing another boy'. There was also confusion over Ned; he was identified as Healey, the stepson of Denis Healey, although he had been sent to the training ship as Donnelly. The Mayor remanded them for a week so that inquiries could be made about the horse and other articles in their possession believed to have been stolen.

There was worse in store for Jack. He was told by the police that on the previous afternoon two of his brothers had been at the lower dam on the Camp Reserve. With the temperature hovering around the century mark, Patrick had been cooling off on a stump at the water's edge. He went over the stump and slipped into deep water where an old cart track had been. He could not swim. Neither could James, who tried to grab him by the hair but failed. James screamed for assistance and a labourer named Power jumped the fence from the street and ran into the water, which came up to his arms. In a few minutes he found

Patrick and dragged him out, but all attempts to resuscitate the boy failed. On receiving the news, Jack appeared to the *Advertiser*'s reporter

> ... to be much affected, and wept bitterly as he was being taken to the gaol. The double calamity must be very hard on the poor parents, whom, we understand, are respectable, industrious people. Nothing could cause feelings of anguish more than the thought that whilst the coroner was holding an inquest on the dead body of one son, the other was standing in the felon's dock charged with one of the most serious crimes against the law, and against society.

The *Advertiser*'s leader on 10 January condemned the episode as 'youthful depravity' and reflected gloomily on the dismal prospects for the colony if it had to rely on such larrikins and larrikinesses as breeding stock. Whipping might serve for the boys but an 'efficient corrective' for the girls would still be lacking.

> Kindly remonstrance being of no avail, and the desire to rise in the social scale seeming to be dead within them, what alternative is there but to subject them to compulsory treatment, and to visit their offences with a degree of severity which may operate in a salutary manner on the fears of the masses?

It was not made clear whether the masses referred to were the youngsters or their respectable elders. Certain it was that in the 1870s social indiscipline among the young was a major public issue, particularly in Melbourne, and thoughtful Victorians were fearful for the future. But then, has it not always been so? The *Advertiser* was sure that parental neglect was the cause of the evil and favoured remedial action by the state, specifically in the form of education, which should be both compulsory and 'attractive'. By attractive it meant 'incentives for self-improvement' and 'inducements ... for exertion on the part of parents to supplement the work of the schoolmaster'. What these might be the paper did not say.

These reflections were the work of the editor of the *Advertiser*, Robert Ross Haverfield. The severity of his views on youthful indiscipline sat uneasily with his reputation as a champion of the underdog. He had founded the *Advertiser* in 1853 for that very purpose, denouncing the heavy-handed and sometimes corrupt officials of the goldfields who were soon to provoke armed resistance at Eureka. In his time he had been stockman, grazier, explorer and digger, and his literary interests were not confined to the newspaper. He contributed stories and verses to many of Melbourne's periodicals as they sprang to life, had their moment and then disappeared. He and Macoboy were as one on the need for exemplary punishment of juvenile offenders and the merits of the birch, but they would have parted company when it came to severity. His more stringent approach might indeed have been a reaction to Macoboy's softer views on sentencing. Haverfield had been editor of Echuca's *Riverine Herald* in 1869, when the judge had been as lenient as he could with the town's 'little bushrangers'. Haverfield was also no doubt familiar with Macoboy's evidence to the Royal Commission, where the judge had set out his reasons for the sentences given in that case.

For Jack and Ned the views of any newspaper editor were academic. Their dice were cast. The only question still to be answered was the nature of the 'compulsory treatment' the state would inflict on them.

A Mother's Anguish

And never rob a mother of her son and only joy
Or else he might turn outlaw like the Wild Colonial Boy

Ned and Jack were back in court in Bendigo on 16 January 1872. So was Judge Macoboy, but the boys were in the Police Court, not his.[44] The police had decided that they were William Jones and James Doolan. The weather was still oppressive, and although the courtroom was stifling at least those present were in shade. The previous day a labourer in the street outside had collapsed with heat stroke. He died even as the court sat. Jack's brother James was stricken in Barnard Street, but after two hours of treatment in the operating room of the hospital he was well enough to be removed to the convalescent ward. The *Advertiser* was convinced that the accumulating misadventures of the three Doolan boys were 'another proof of the strange fatality which sometimes follow[s] the children of some families.'[45]

There were four charges: breaking, entering and stealing from Hehir's house; stealing Steer's horse; armed robbery of widow Foley; and stealing under arms from Hallinan. Davidson had found Bridget Foley's billy cans in the bush, where the boys had hidden or abandoned them, and she had been found and persuaded to give evidence. She told her story in a straightforward fashion to the court, asserting that *both* boys had presented firearms at her. Ned cross-examined her: what were these firearms? 'A pistol or revolver', Bridget replied, 'not a gun'. So there was only one weapon, but this was a trivial inconsistency as far as the court was concerned.

The other victims were called. Hehir was sworn and Davidson led Ned from the dock to the front of the bench so that the miner could identify the clothes that the boy was wearing. Ned struggled and cursed and tried to box with the officer. It was a bit late to be offering resistance. Hehir said that Ned was wearing some of his clothes. Steer identified his horse, which should have been sufficient for the court's purposes, but his daughter Eveline

Ned Donnelly, accomplice of the Wild Colonial Boy. PROV, VPRS 515, Central Prisoner Records Males, Unit 14, No. 9557. Keeper of Public Records, Public Record Office, Victoria

was also called. She testified that the horse had gone missing before 2 January. She admitted that she knew Ned, by the name of Healey, and had seen Jack. It was perhaps being implied that she was involved in the removal of the horse, but there was no follow up. Hallinan identified his cart. He too knew Ned, but by the name of Donnelly.[46] What he did not volunteer was that Ned's mother, before she married, was also a Hallinan. No wonder Ned had known where he might find a cart; the man who had tracked him was almost certainly a relative – his uncle, his cousin, or even his grandfather.

In the determined and successful attempts by the prosecution to identify all the stolen property there is a glaring omission. No-one asked how two adolescents came to have a loaded revolver, or whose it was. It might have been William Dooling's; most diggers had gone armed during the 1850s. Or was it a Hallinan weapon whose loss could not be admitted without raising awkward questions about family relationships? The bench was not much interested. Neither of the boys made a statement to the court, which might have exposed the issue. There was no option this time of sending the case to Judge Macoboy in the Court of General Sessions. The boys were committed for trial by the Circuit Court in February, Ned on all four counts, Jack only on three because luckily he had not been wearing any of Hehir's clothes when arrested, although he had quite likely been present when they were stolen. The newspaper roundsmen did their best to prejudice the boys' chances of getting a fair hearing before a jury.

> Jones, who is about 17, seems to be a determined scoundrel, and Doolan, who is about a year younger,

47

has a bad look, though he seemed to feel his position more acutely.[47]

Jones is a desperate character and wants taming; if such a rascal had been allowed to escape the police for any length of time he would have become a most audacious scoundrel.[48]

Two days later the editor of the *News* returned to the case. He had decided that the boys were a new type of criminal – 'Larrikin Bushrangers'.

The boys Doolan and Jones ... developments of the species Larrikin ... are not very creditable to our social states or the district. The conduct of these imps in bailing up and robbing widow Foley presents features of exceptional depravity ... Such cases should furnish *prima facie* evidence sufficient to influence the Government to take prompt and energetic action, immediately upon the reassembling of Parliament, for the suppression of larrikinism. As we have before indicated, we believe that whipping and the stocks will be found the most effectual mode of reducing the evil.

He warned the politicians that opposition to such measures would be open to criticism as 'conniving at criminality'. Presumably the criticism would be coming from newspaper editors, and perhaps them alone, for in the very next line he conceded that political opposition would be for the base purpose of currying popularity. Action was imperative if Victoria was not to go the way of America.

Larrikinism is the cradle of criminality, and a prolific germ of those abnormal social or class excrescences with which America has been afflicted. It is essentially a movement that should be nipped in the bud. It has al-

> ready been allowed too much development, and its fur-
> ther toleration is a premium to crime ... It will doubt-
> less require some stringent legislation to suppress and
> put down these inchoate fillibusters – the larrikins. [49]

For a month the boys languished in custody, locked up during one of the hottest summers that anyone could recall. Their trial, on 19 February, was brief. They were brought up before Supreme Court Justice Edward Eyre Williams and a jury of twelve. Ned pleaded guilty. Jack pleaded not guilty, perhaps hoping that he might avoid conviction on the most serious charges, robbery under arms, as there was no evidence that he had wielded the revolver. But he had been present when Ned did, and that was enough. Both boys were convicted as charged and remanded for sentence.

Two days later Justice Williams pronounced. He was grieved, he said, to see before him two young boys (he thought that they were 13 and 14) charged with such a long catalogue of crimes. It seemed as if they were full-fledged bushrangers, using pistols with the same freedom as sugar plums. When society saw such young ruffians spring up in its midst, the strong arm of the law had to nip their careers in the bud. He assured them that it would be a long time before they again had liberty to abuse, and could endanger the lives of peaceable people. For horse stealing, two years; for robbery under arms of the cart, six years; for robbery under arms of a dwelling, six years; and for Ned, additionally, three years for breaking into Hehir's house. With hard labour. Cumulative. The boys took their medicine in silence, without any sign of remorse or emotion: to the *Advertiser*'s reporter they looked 'as hardened as old and daring convicts'.[50]

But there was a stir in the court. Everyone knew that Harry Power, who claimed to have committed hundreds of offences during his last period at large and had been convicted on three counts of bushranging, had got only fifteen years. And this was after cheeking the bench, promising the judge that if he 'drew it mild' Power would be lenient with him should they subsequently meet in the bush![51] The boy Jones was being given two years more than Power and young Doolan only slightly less. What followed was variously described by the newspaper reporters as 'a heartrending shriek' or 'a piercing lamentation'. Ann Dooling, who had sat silently throughout the committal proceedings and trial, was now standing in the body of the court giving vent to her grief. For several minutes the business of the court could not proceed. Amid 'great commotion' and an 'affecting scene' the distraught mother was removed from the courthouse. She was 'tottering feebly', 'almost dementedly' crying over and over, 'Oh my boy, my poor boy.' Even the hard case from the *Evening Star* was affected.

> The parents of this truly unfortunate lad would appear to have drunk deeply of affliction, as not only is this, their eldest son, sent into a banishment with scarcely a prospect of ever seeing him again, but it will be remembered that they lost another son, who was drowned in the reserve some short time since, and more recently still another of their sons was afflicted.[52]

Editorial opinion was mixed. The *Independent* thought that the length of the sentences for these 'young desperadoes' would be a salutary warning to the youth of the colony. The sympathies of others lay more with the boys while allowing Justice Williams benefit of the doubt. The *Evening News* referred to Ned's threat to rape widow Foley, and thought that might account for the judge's severity. It was concerned, however, that Jack would be going to prison for 'a term of years about equal to the number he has lived', and was of the view that

> A sound flogging or two, and a month's imprisonment, would probably have operated with a better moral effect upon the lad, and with a more deterring influence as an example to others.[53]

No similar solicitude was expressed for Ned, but then his mother had not provided such spectacularly melodramatic copy. In the *Advertiser* Haverfield was torn. His paper was on record as favouring corporal punishment rather than prison sentences, but corporal punishment was not an option open to the judge. While 'strongly disposed' to quarrel with the length of the sentences, Haverfield was anxious to consider both sides of the question. The boys were, according to all the accounts, 'hardened and apparently incorrigible rascals'; clemency would have been wasted.

> Society demanded not only that it should be relieved of the great annoyance of their delinquencies, but also of the fearful example set by them to the youth of the neighbourhoods they infested. Certainly, the judge had no alternative but to send them to jail for lengthy periods.[54]

The question of example may have been closer to the mark than he realized. On the day that Justice Williams tried the boys he also had before him another juvenile horse thief, William Sibley. Sibley had borrowed a horse for two hours but had failed to return it. Two days later he had been arrested on the road to

Swan Hill. Because the horse had been 'borrowed', not stolen outright, the charge was larceny as a bailee and Williams was constrained in sentencing. Sibley got four years.[55] The judge would have known that in the eyes of the public the offence would be indistinguishable from horse stealing. Four years was not a strong message if one subscribed to the Macoboy theory that epidemic crime required ruthless deterrence. It is possible that Ned and Jack got harder sentences than they might have had Williams been able to make more of an example of Sibley.[56] Haverfield, however, considered the boys' case in isolation and concluded that the sentences were excessive.

> The crimes of which the boys were convicted, as well as their vicious and dangerous habits of life, necessitated their incarceration and exclusion from the world for prolonged periods. But the span of human life is brief at the longest and ever uncertain. Much shorter terms, therefore, than those of fourteen and seventeen years are [still] comparatively long, and the impressions that may be received during even one year will have a very serious effect on the minds and characters of very young persons. In consigning a lad for any period to gaol we are perpetuating the principal means of his ruin, by throwing him into bad company ... we cannot forget that in casting a youth into the companionship of criminals for the greater part of his life, we are cutting him off from all hope of reclamation.

Like the reporters, Haverfield made much of Ann Dooling's cry while denying any 'sentimental mood.' The judge, he wrote, must surely have been struck to his heart and

> ... The wild and despairing wail, 'My poor boy!' should find an echo in quarters in which the young criminal

can claim neither kith nor kin by the ties of blood. The country to which a life, which might be made valuable to it, has been utterly and irretrievably lost, may well cry aloud 'poor boy'; and some strenuous effort should be made for the redemption of such children of ignorance and sin.

In the meantime, if they could not be whipped 'as they ought to be – not with the disgusting cat, brutally lacerating their bodies, but with some more appropriate instrument' they should receive some 'corporal chastening'. Hard labour would not do; the labour was not hard and prisoners doing it were fed on the highest scale of rations. Better that the current 'hard labour' be intermittent, with reduced rations during the intervals. Let them laugh at and make light of prison life then! As for Ned and Jack, they

> ... have gone, for the best part of their lives, where they will neither be radically reformed nor effectually punished; and when at last they receive their liberty, they will be cast loose upon society confirmed gaol birds, reckless of themselves, hating the world, despising its laws, and ever ready to brave those worst consequences of crime to which they have become thoroughly inured.[57]

It was not a Damascene conversion but it was a shift. A mother's tears had prompted Haverfield, the scourge of larrikinism, to reconsider the efficacy and humanity of his prescriptions.

The Makings of a Legend

He bade the Judge 'Good morning', and told him to beware,
That he'd never rob a hearty chap that acted on the square.

The day after Jack and Ned were sentenced, James Doolan was caught trying to steal from a shop in View Place, near his home. The shop owner declined to charge an eight-year-old and sent him home with a request that he be punished. The *Advertiser* was filled with foreboding; 'it is to be hoped that he will not follow in the footsteps of his brother'.[58] A week later James was arrested for stealing a birdcage.[59] Ann Dooling could not face the court. She sent her daughter Catherine, nineteen, to represent the family.

James's cause would have been better served had Catherine stayed at home. The girl might have been disturbed at the effect the succession of disasters was having on the mental state of her mother. The cycle had to be broken. Catherine told the court that her brother had been let off only days earlier; his family could not correct him. The bench acted on this character reference; three days' imprisonment, to be followed by five years on the training ship. The court later summonsed William Dooling to contribute to the upkeep of his son while in custody, which was the usual arrangement, but the case was dismissed when William proved that he was unemployed and had no money to give.[60] It was a reasonable excuse for one kind of dereliction but exposed another. If he had no employment what excuse had he for neglecting to supervise and control his sons? The Royal Commission's suggested solution was no answer; a father who could not financially support his son was unlikely to be able to pay a fine for neglecting him. 'The Last of the Doolans', the *Advertiser* called James, as if it were the end of an outlaw dynasty.[61] For Ann Dooling, having lost three sons in seven weeks, it must have seemed the end of her family.

Because of official confusion about Jack's name, James was initially admitted to Pentridge before the authorities there noticed that they now had two James Doolans and one of them was a bit young even by their standards. They redirected him to the reformatory, which noted that he had '2 sisters and 3 brothers, one of whom (John Doolan) is sentenced to 14 years in Pentridge for bushranging'.[62] But Pentridge did not alter its records and so, until the last trump sounds, Jack will be James (the elder) to the Victorian penal system.

The boys were in gaol, but controversy sputtered on in Bendigo. Haverfield delivered himself of one last broadside, this time not against but on behalf of 'Our Youthful Criminals'.

> No enemy has sown the tares springing up so rankly among our wheat. The damage that has been done is the work of our own hands. And while we look on shocked and amazed at the extent of the mischief, we still stand with folded arms making no attempt at reparation … We have made fine work truly for the turnkey, the flogger and the hangman. There is not the smallest fear of any of these callings dying out or growing rusty. It is a pleasant and humane task certainly to employ ourselves constantly in the knotting of whips.

Thus the former advocate of the lash. 'The only real and radical cure for larrikinism', Haverfield went on, was compulsory education, even if it meant children being given religious instruction outside of their parents' faith.[63]

His leader prompted a couple of letters to the editor and a petition was got up against the severity of the sentences but, when all was said and done, it was a one week wonder. Whence then, from such unpromising material, came the inspiration for a ballad? The answer to that question depends on what kind of ballad one is looking for. The material was less than promising for a bushranging ballad, but perhaps *Wild Colonial Boy* did not begin life as bushranging ballad. To understand how that might have been it is necessary to review some features of public life in the Bendigo of the early 1870s.

Gold gave Bendigo a continuing prosperity that few other Victorian country centres could boast. It was proclaimed a city in 1871 but, for all that, it was still a provincial town. The council and the police court were the founts of most local news and both were closely scrutinized by a vigorous press. Two morning and two evening newspapers competed for the business of local advertisers and there was a satirical sheet called *Pasquin* that circulated nightly in 'all the principal places of amusement'. Foremost amongst these was the Lyceum Theatre, a Pall Mall venue capable of seating 2000, whose stage had been graced by all the famous entertainers of the era from Charles Kean to G. V. Brooke. By the end of 1871 the Lyceum's owner, Joseph Abbott, Jack's former master, had decided that retailers would make more reliable tenants than theatrical folk. The theatre was scheduled for closure or, as the *Advertiser* put it,

Thalia would be retired in favour of Plutus. This was a blow to the particular theatrical who had been lessee of the Lyceum on and off since 1869.

Harry Stanley was an itinerant comic who in 1865 had played a minor part in the first Australian production of Boucicault's *Arrah-na-Pogue*. He had danced the barn door jig that preceded the 'rebel's song', *Wearing of the Green*, and in subsequent years had made a modest name for himself in the harlequinades that were a feature of Melbourne's Christmas pantomimes. Then, even more than now, the pantomime was a vehicle for satire, for 'hits' at prominent persons and current events in parodies of popular songs ('local subjects plentifully interspersed and liberally treated by everybody'). '*Arrah-na-Poger*' itself had been given the treatment at Christmas 1865 in the pantomime *Baron Munchausen*.[64]

When Stanley took up the lease of the Lyceum he brought with him a company of Melbourne players that included his wife, and for three years Bendigo was not dependent on touring companies for professional theatre. The staple fare was comedy, farce and burlesque, interspersed with more serious pieces. Bendigo had already seen a touring company's production of *Arrah-na-Pogue*. The critic for the *News* had thought it a 'very interesting Irish Dramma' but had been at a loss to account for the pit being so crammed that some could not gain admission and many who did could not obtain sitting room. Their insistence on an encore of *Wearing of the Green* might have given him a hint but he was not about to acknowledge any rebel sentiment or even that most of those jammed shoulder to shoulder in the pit would have been Irish diggers.[65] Stanley was more sensitive to his audience.

Wearing of the Green became his standard concert piece and he even inserted it into his production of another Boucicault play, *The Colleen Bawn*.[66]

Wearing of the Green became a favorite in Bendigo. In 1870 the Boucicault lyrics were printed in the poetry column of the *News*.[67] Stanley also wrote his own local comic songs. They were of the moment and none of them survives, but one was entitled *Hact on the Square*, a phrase that occurs in *Wild Colonial Boy*. It was 'much relished' and twice encored on debut.[68] For his swan song at the Lyceum Stanley went back to pantomime. At Christmas 1871 he mounted *Sinbad the Sailor*, promising several local hits such as *A Bedroom on Sandhurst* and *The Shamrock Hotel*, 'etc., etc.'.[69] The show was a great success and in January he took it on tour to the nearby towns. It opened in Castlemaine on the day that Constable Davidson put an end to the bushranging careers of Jack and Ned. The reviewer for the *Mount Alexander Mail* was enthusiastic.

> The piece abounds with local hits and smart repartees, and the popular melodies interspersed throughout render it at once acceptable to those who seek for a good evening's entertainment.[70]

As every performance was different the reviewer was back on the second night, when he found the local hits to be nicely judged: 'well told, not too openly, but just sufficient to rouse the risible faculties'. Alas, he gave no hint as to the topics 'hit'. It might have just been a coincidence but the *Mail* chose just then to editorialize on the 'larrikin epidemic'. Alas, it cited no examples of the disease.[71]

Dedicated to the
Fenian Brotherhood

"Wearing of the Green"

As Sung by
J. E. MᶜDONOUGH
IN
E. H. House & Dion Boucicault's
CELEBRATED IRISH DRAMA OF
ARRAH NA POGUE

PHILADELPHIA
Published by Chas W A Trumpler 77 & Chestnut St

Boucicault's dedication of Wearing of the Green to the Fenians. Keffer Collection, Penn Library

When Stanley returned to Bendigo he was given a farewell benefit. On 31 January, the last night of his management, he did scenes from *Colleen Bawn* and danced the Barn Door Jig. Seven weeks later he repeated the performance at a charity benefit where he was reported to have sung *Wearing of the Green* 'with unusual vigor and feeling'.[72] It might have been another coincidence but in the interval between the two performances Bendigo's most distinguished Irishman, Judge Macoboy, had finally succumbed after a long illness. The closest the liberal jurist had come to an encounter with Jack Doolan was in the reporting of their various doings in adjacent columns of the local newspapers.[73]

Circumstantial evidence is seldom satisfying, and the several activities of Jack Doolan, William Davidson, Robert Haverfield, Harry Stanley and Michael Macoboy in Bendigo in the summer of 1872 do not mesh with any certainty. The best verdict that could be expected of a disinterested jury would be 'not proven'. Yet the main cast of *Wild Colonial Boy* is assembled, its tune is in the air, an opinion maker is changing his mind in public and an impresario who pokes fun at local absurdities is trying to make a living. This is the stuff of satire.

If one looks at *Wild Colonial Boy* through the distorting lens of the satirist some things becomes clearer. Two boys have been sent to prison for a long time, and for what? It is not as though they have done anything really serious, like sticking up the Beechworth mail *à la* Harry Power. How much harm did they do with their 'little toy' – did they try to shoot it out with the police? No, they were overawed. So how many police did it take to disarm this outlaw band – three, four? Well, just the one – but the judge must have known what he was doing. Oh yes, like reducing Doolan's mother to despair: old Macoboy, rest his soul, would never have been that harsh. If he had been on the case, and true to his principles, neither of the boys would have got more than six years. And so on.

There are hints of Jack's story in the song. The reference to the pistol as a little toy echoes Williams' comparison of it to a sugarplum. Concern for the bushranger's mother is a central element in both the newspaper stories and the song. Deconstruction of the names in the song also casts some light.

What if Macoboy is not an actor in the drama but just a well-known local judge whose name, unlike Williams, rhymes with 'boy'? In the song Jack is wounded/captured/killed by Kelly, Davis and Fitzroy. Kelly was the alias used by Jack when arrested by Davi[d]s[on]. Fitzroy is another convenient rhyme for 'boy', and the Melbourne suburb of that name was a hotbed of larrikinism. Macoboy did not have jurisdiction anywhere near *Beech*worth, but *Rush*worth was on his Bendigo circuit. The real tease is Castlemaine. Is it again just a convenient rhyme, in this case for 'name', or is it a localism from the time Harry Stanley's troupe took their pantomime to that town? If neither, how is it that the Boy's birthplace is correct, given that this fact was known only to his family, the penal system and perhaps those present in court in 1869 when Martley produced the family bible?[74] None of this gives us a ballad maker, but these are surely a ballad's makings.

Fourteen Years Hard

*There is not a life in all of the records of the past, but, properly
studied, might lend a hint and a help to some contemporary.*
Robert Louis Stevenson

Happy is the historian whose subject goes to gaol. The state in its
custodial role is particularly intrusive. It captures and preserves
the lives of ordinary people whose personal histories might
otherwise be lost. Without the state's need to account for those
in its custody, the life of many an individual subsequently found
to be worthy of study would be no more recoverable than a wave
that has spent itself on the shore.

Admission to Pentridge was like nothing so much as induction
into a monastic order, whose novices were expected to observe
silence and solitary repentance as the order of the day. All traces
of individuality were hidden by prison garb and, whenever in the
presence of one's fellows, by a full-face linen mask. Two eyeholes
were the only features on its blank, anonymous surface. One of
the changes advocated by the Royal Commission on Penal and
Prison Discipline was that prisoners should be photographed for
identification purposes.[75] Although Jack and Ned were amongst
the earliest prisoners to be so recorded, for them it was too late
to achieve its intended purpose. The system itself had already
in effect given them false identities. James Doolan, as he had

become, was set down as 5'1" tall, 7 stones 12½ pounds in weight, with sallow complexion, dark brown hair, brown eyes and a freckled face. A feature not apparent from his photograph, indicating that the camera too could mislead, was that his upper teeth were 'prominent'. The buck-toothed lad also had several scars on his left thumb, legacy of his trade.[76]

The rule in Pentridge was that a new prisoner spent his first months, to a maximum of nine, separately confined in A Division. Not yet sixteen, Jack was shut up by himself for 23 hours in the day. The other hour was for outdoor exercise, taken alone in a caged run under the eye of a warder from whose elevated central

WAITING FOR EXAMINAITON.

The separate and silent system, Pentridge. *Illustrated Australian News*, 27 August 1867. National Library of Australia

post fourteen identical runs radiated outwards on the panopticon principle. While passing under escort from and to his cell in the company of others Jack wore his mask. The normal employment for novices was light work such as plaiting straw for hats, but there is some evidence that Jack was allowed to make shoes. The daily ration, while less than for those at hard labour, was adequate; 16 ounces of bread, 8 of maize or oats, 8 of potatoes, 6 of meat, an ounce of sugar and a half an ounce of salt.[77]

Jack did not take well to the disciplines of A Division. In his period of separate confinement he chalked up thirteen offences, mainly in attempts to communicate with other prisoners. In some of these he was successful for at various times he was found to have tobacco and papers 'with writing' and 'obscene drawings' in his possession. He was not cowed; in July 1872 he was caught 'talking, whistling and dancing' in his cell. That earned him two days' solitary, which as he was already in separate confinement meant bread and water in a punishment cell; underground, totally devoid of light, sleeping on the bare floor. His longest stint in solitary was ten days, but even that was insufficient for his worst offence. He threatened to stab an officer with a knife, presumably one issued to him for cobbling. The visiting justice gave him two months in irons for that indiscretion. By the standards of the old days the seven-pound chains around his ankles were no great imposition. Within a week or two he would have been walking as freely in them as a gent in his pumps. It says little for the commonsense of the prison authorities that the boy who had stabbed John Zahner was given access to a knife so early in his sentence. While it is true that all they knew of his previous record was that he had been in reformatory for 'inflicting bodily injury', no less a personage than the Superintendent of Pentridge was on record as agreeing that the majority of serious offences in prison were committed by persons of sedentary occupations.

> I would allude particularly to shoemakers – they are very apt to use the knife, and passionately attack one another with it. Tailors and shoe-makers, I think give more trouble than other classes of prisoners.[78]

Jack's poor record in A Division was counted against him. After his allotted time in separate confinement was up[79] he was told that when his sentence neared expiry he would be allowed to submit a 'claim for consideration'. The claim would be for remission, available as a reward for good conduct after two-thirds of a sentence had expired. But to the two-thirds qualifying period were added the terms of all punishments for misconduct while in prison, and Jack already had three months' worth of those. He would have at least nine years more to serve. In the second phase of his imprisonment Jack was put to what passed for hard labour. The unskilled and unskilful might break rocks or even, in the phrase so beloved of judges, be put to work on the roads, but in B Division so far as possible the skilled laboured at their trades and the unskilled with potential were assisted to acquire one. At night Jack was put in a separate cell but in the workshop and at meals he associated with the other prisoners. Silence was still enforced but exception was made on the subject of work. In the shoemaking shop, with one overseer in charge of sixty or seventy prisoners, the concession made for lively traffic as illicit footwear was traded for tobacco and other contraband. And, as the *Bendigo Advertiser* had feared, Jack's meat and potato rations were doubled and he got an extra four ounces of bread.

SOLITARY CONFINEMENT.

A Division cell, Pentridge. *Australasian Sketcher*, 4 October 1873. National Library of Australia

The bell rang at seven in the morning. Twenty minutes was allowed for breakfast and by 7.30 Jack would be at work in his stall. At 11.45 the prisoners were summoned to dinner. They were searched on leaving the workshop and marched to the mess hall, returning to the workshop at 12.55. Work ceased at 4.15 pm. There was an hour of school, followed by supper and lockdown at 6 pm except for those attending evening school in the mess room. By the standards of the 1870s it was a very short working day and productivity was low. Even a trained shoemaker like Jack would make only three pairs of Blucher boots a week.[80]

The offences that Jack committed in B Division reflected the greater relative freedom he enjoyed there. The range of contraband he was caught with expanded; boxing gloves and handkerchiefs, for example, and, more seriously, knives and a small steel saw. He was charged at various times with being insolent and disobedient to those in authority over him, and with assaulting and threatening other prisoners. He was occasionally on the receiving end, in 1875 being assaulted by one Sullivan, 'the Yarra Flats bushranger'. Far from expressing sympathy, the *Argus* implied that it was deserved, Jack being 'one of about thirty of the worst prisoners in Pentridge'.[81]

Over the three years 1873–75 Jack had committed twenty punishable offences, the worst of which, the assault, earned him twenty days in solitary. All up, he had set his remission back another 69 days. At the end of 1875, however, when he was nineteen, a change came over his behaviour. Six months passed before he again offended. It would be nice to ascribe this to a new maturity or at least to a sensible determination to keep his head down, but the probable explanation is less creditable: it is about this time that he would have been eligible for transfer to C Division.

C Division was Pentridge's social club. Prisoners were supposed to go there after divisions A and B had wrought their 'moral effect' and reform was well under way. Ideally, all prisoners would have seen out their sentences in B Division, but it was not large enough. In C Division, prisoners continued to sleep in individual cells but they associated at work, at meals and during recreation. Communication was unrestrained and transfer to C was thought to undo whatever good might have been achieved in the other two divisions.

In C Division Jack and Ned would have been able to associate freely for the first time in four years. Ned had behaved no better than Jack in the early part of his sentence. He had committed only 14 offences to Jack's 34 but his had included two assaults on prison officers that between them had cost him ten months' remission. Now both of them found it easier to avoid detection, and punishment, under the slacker regimen of C Division. Jack even had a change of air; for three months at the end of 1876 he was sent to Geelong for restoration work on the gaol. But prison life was eating away at him. In 1880 he again began to offend more frequently, culminating in an escape attempt. That August he tried to tunnel out through the floor of his cell and excavated over half a ton of soil before being detected. The visiting justice gave him four months' hard labour in irons, and it is safe to assume that for once at least Jack found himself working in the stoneyard. It seems to have had the desired effect. Apart from once being caught smoking and at another time found 'impertinent' for writing a letter (one outwards every three months was the ration), Jack had a clean slate for the rest of his sentence.

The Royal Commission had recommended individual cells for C Division prisoners for the same reason that it disapproved of the lack of segregation on the training ship. Its concern about the crime that dares not tell its name raises the question of how a handsome youngster like Jack fared in the company of older men who, even if not committed for sexual offences – and many were – were sexually deprived. In 1876 an *Argus* journalist,

John Stanley James, who published under the pseudonym The Vagabond, spent a month undercover in the prison hospital.

> ... at Pentridge there still remains a vestige of those offences which, in these columns, I scarcely dare hint at, but which Mr Marcus Clark boldly alludes to in *His Natural Life*. The discovery of this, and a horrible 'ring', was most revolting to me, and I can never sufficiently express my detestation of the damnable system which allows comparatively innocent youths to be mixed up with wretches perpetually sinning against God and man. The offences for which many prisoners are committed are those which should make them a class by themselves, never under any pretense being allowed to mingle with the rest.[82]

Jack's prison record reveals no evidence one way or the other, but his serial punishments for quarrelling and threatening behaviour, not to mention his ability to lay his hands on knives and the like from time to time, and his conviction for stabbing in 1869, might well have persuaded the predators that there were safer targets. Ned's record is not quite as clean. In 1881 he was 'found in his cell with a prisoner'. There is no indication that they were caught having sex; indeed, Ned's punishment of three months' hard labour is evidence that he was not caught *in flagrante delicto*.[83] If so he would have been flogged, 'unnatural crime' being one of the few offences still to attract the lash.[84]

John Doolan, 26, free by remission. PROV, VPRS 515, Central Prisoner Records Males, Unit 14, No. 9556. Keeper of Public Records, Public Records Office, Victoria

The Ballad of Jack Doolan

Air: *The Wearing of the Green* or *The Wild Colonial Boy*

Jack's real career would have been of little interest to the Kelly sympathizers. It is also too short on glamour for the likes of Henry Lawson's Flash Jack, who sang *Wild Colonial Boy* resplendent in 'red sash, cabbagetree hat on back of head with nothing in it, glossy black curls bunched up in front of brim'.[85] Those looking to associate themselves with the mystique of the Boy would find it hard to embrace a ballad that faithfully described his bushranging career. After all, it would have to be something like …

> There was a wild colonial boy, John Doolan was his name
> Of poor dishonest parents, he was born in Castlemaine.
> He was his father's second son, his parents' pride and joy,
> And dearly did his mother love her wild colonial boy.
>
> Come all you wild colonial boys, we'll roam the mountains high,
> Together we will plunder, together we will die.
> We'll wander over valleys, and gallop over plains,
> And scorn to slave our lives away, with poverty for chains.
>
> In sixty-nine this daring youth began his wild career,
> He stuck his knife in Zahner's son and gave a rousing cheer.
> To kill him were no harm, Jack cried, for me he did annoy,
> Still shy of thirteen years he was, our wild colonial boy.

He called me Irish pig and thief, I'll take that from no French,
And no more boots I'll make with him beside me at the bench.
His mother she did fear for Jack and tears her eyes did cloy,
The day her 'prentice lad became a wild colonial boy.

The wound is slight, no grievous harm, old doctor Betham said.
No grievous harm? the Bench demurred, why Zahner might be dead.
This case goes to the Circuit Court and not to Macoboy,
Sir William Stawell's the man who'll try this wild colonial boy.

He's just a boy, for mercy's sake, the Sandhurst jury begged,
But Justice Stawell was well resolved to take Jack down a peg.
A twelve-month cruise in Hobson's Bay is what you will enjoy,
Sir Harry Smith will make of you a mild colonial boy.

The year goes by and unreformed, Jack's back in Bendigo,
The papers there they do complain 'Bushranging's all the go.
The lure of easy gold, we find, youth's morals do destroy',
Why there's a flash idea, thought he, the wild colonial boy.

Old Harry Power was long at large and robbed the Beechworth mail,
But troopers three took him at last and he's in Pentridge gaol.
The highway's free and here I am, a lad none will employ,
That vacancy I'll fill, as I'm a wild colonial boy.

Although not yet of sixteen years he left his father's home,
And through the streets of Bendigo in early hours did roam,
To burn the Beehive brokers' mart and all their stocks destroy.
Or was it brother James become a wild colonial boy?

Bill Jones and Jack on New Year's Eve robbed Widow Foley's place,
The swag was only three and six, a bushranging disgrace.
'No more than half a crown we'll lift without a better ploy,
A horse, a horse, we'll get', quoth he, the wild colonial boy.

So down to Axedale they did go to take Steer's chestnut steed,
But one horse 'twixt the two of them was less than what they'd need.

And Hallinan's spring cart, they felt, they'd get without much noise,
Our horse before that cart must go, say wild colonial boys.

At Hallinan's they looked around for harness and for reins.
A stable hand yelled 'What the h…?' Jack said, 'Blow out his brains!'
'Only if he says a word' – Bill Jones had kept his poise –
They wouldn't want to swing for it, the wild colonial boys.

So what's next, boys? A bank? A train? Perhaps the Rushworth mail?
It might as well be big, says Jack, my dad cannot go bail.
We'll not be caught and if we are we'll hope for Macoboy,
Because, said Bill, he's like to spare a wild colonial boy.

The White Hills road that morning saw them whip their horse along,
All heedless of the warning in the kookaburra's song.
A single trooper hove in sight (no Kellys or Fitzroys),
'Twas Davidson who ran them down, the wild colonial boys.

The trooper's horse was fresh as paint but Steer's they had to spell,
It pulled up blown outside – no lie – the Robin Hood Hotel.
Cool Davidson's Crimea trained, two pistols he deploys,
So will they act like children now, or wild colonial boys?

Surrender now, Jack Doolan, although I'm one 'gainst two,
Surrender in the Queen's name for my duty I will do.
Jack had his pistol pocketed, but dared not draw the toy,
He'd rather live than die, would he, this wild colonial boy.

The charges 'fore the magistrates were robbery under arms,
Horse-stealing, theft, bad language, youth, and sundry like alarms.
It's too rich for this Bench, they cried, and as for Macoboy,
Again he'll miss his chance to try the wild colonial boy.

It grieves me sore, Judge Williams said, this catalogue of crime,
A Colt is not a sugar plum and you'll do Pentridge time.
And do not think your tender years my purpose will decoy,
It's porridge hard and long for you, my wild colonial boy.

The Circuit Court was light on Jack, he got just fourteen years,
But Bill, who had a bit more form, got three more for arrears.
Jack's mother wept and prayed for less, but there she had no joy,
And at the sentence she did cry 'My poor colonial boy!'

A modern lout, the papers said, does not bush range at all,
He fights beneath the town's gas lights, accosts girls in the Mall.
But prison is crime's crucible and Jack it might alloy,
To make a hardened street thug of our wild colonial boy.

This many years we've searched for him, a hero of the bush,
And what does he turn out to be? Apprenticed to the push!
For here there is no bold outlaw, Dick Turpin or Rob Roy,
A larrikin from Bendigo's our wild colonial boy.

The moral of Jack's story is, and sad it is to tell,
Put not your trust in ballads if you'd drink at Clio's well.
Their rhymes will leave you all amazed, and reason they'll destroy,
By mixing fact with fiction 'bout the wild colonial boy.

But all you true Australians, who'd roam the mountains high,
Who'd claim the freedom of the bush, authority defy!
And keep alive the other tale that's long been sung of Jack,
For legends are in short supply, and that's a cold hard fact.

An Unfortunate Family

… the strange fatality that follows the children of some families.
Bendigo Advertiser

On 13 August 1882 Jack walked out of Pentridge a free man. He had served ten and a half years at a time when only 6% of Victorian prisoners received sentences of longer than ten years, and with remission many did not serve their full tariff.[86] To a youngster it must have seemed an unimaginably long time. While he had been counting off the weary years Ned Kelly had done his time in Pentridge, become the terror of Victoria, been pursued, taken, tried and hanged. At 26 Jack was only 2½ inches taller than when admitted but strong and wiry. His discharge photograph shows that in place of an anxious boy the world was getting a self-confident and perhaps mildly resentful man. Combs as well as food appear to have been rationed in Pentridge. The overall effect is, in a word, wild. He is dressed in a new suit of clothing, value £2/4/6, and has in his pocket £4/18/1, the gratuity for a decade's work. The prison has reported his conduct to the Discharged Prisoners' Aid Society as 'good of late', which would have inclined it to give him a railway pass or tradesman's tools, but he has scorned to apply.[87] He has no need of either. There is nothing for him in Bendigo; his family has moved to Melbourne. He does not intend to practice the trade that got him into trouble in the first place; he will start afresh in a different line of business. He will not reoffend, confounding the fears of those who had predicted that prison would blight his life.[88]

A few months earlier Arthur Hodgson had immortalised him in print in the place of his birth, but already the connection between Boy and Song was so tenuous that the publisher had set his name down as Jack Dowling. Is it coincidence that about this time the family members, Jack included, begin to call themselves Dowling? Or is it because they are trying to reclaim what they regard as a badge of honour? Certainly the family reputation had not improved since Jack had been put away. Its members had faced one trial after another, sometimes literally. In ancient times their misadventures would have been blamed on divine displeasure, but that would have been uncharitable to Fortuna. Most of the Dooling/Doolan/Dowling wounds were self-inflicted.

In September 1872 one John Brunnock was indicted for maliciously wounding Jack's mother Ann. Evidence was given by her daughter Catherine and other witnesses that when she had ordered Brunnock from her house in Barnard Street he had become violent, assaulted her, knocked her down and thrown a stone which had struck her on the head, severely injuring her. She had been taken to the hospital where she had remained in a critical state for several weeks. The wounds had not been dangerous but a serious infection, erysipelas had set in.

Brunnock's counsel attacked Ann: she was the keeper of a disreputable place frequented by 'low characters' and her injuries had been aggravated by her 'mode of living' as she did not seek medical assistance until three or four days after the incident. The injuries were probably caused by her husband, with whom she was 'not on the best of terms'. The barrister also called into question the character of Catherine, inviting the jury to consider if her appearance in the box inspired confidence in her reliability. The Crown Prosecutor perversely endorsed this negative perception by calling her 'unfortunate … and perhaps more an object of sympathy and pity than of contempt and derision', the implication being that Catherine's dress and demeanor stamped her as a prostitute. A boy testified that he had seen Dooling assaulting Ann and that Brunnock had been too drunk to be capable of assaulting anyone. Another witness testified that some days later, at the Filbin premises, he had heard Ann tell Brunnock that if he would 'settle the case' with money she would clear out to Melbourne on next morning's first train. The prosecution would then have collapsed. Although Brunnock had agreed, stipulating that he would not pay directly but through 'any respectable man' in Bendigo, the deal must have fallen through. The jury deliberated at length and found Brunnock not guilty. He was released but both he and Ann were lucky not to have been charged with conspiring to pervert the course of justice.[89]

Ann was in court again a year later, this time with son Thomas, charged with having stolen firewood from the Royal Hustler's mining company one Sunday night. When challenged by a watchman engaged specifically for the purpose of curtailing a spate of thefts, Ann had called him 'a [expletive deleted] scavenger' and threatened to have someone deal with him. Thomas, said to be twelve[90], stepped up and said he would put a knife through him, but both Doolings ran away when the watchman called for assistance. The mine manager asked only for such punishment as would serve as a warning and the bench obliged. Ann and Thomas were sentenced to seven days' imprisonment for larceny.[91]

Having undergone the family initiation, as it were, Thomas became a miner but again ran foul of the law in 1875, when he was arrested for passing a counterfeit coin for pie and coffee at a street stall. His older brother William had done the same to pay for boot repairs but had sensibly decamped for Melbourne. A search of their home in Barnard Street revealed bottles of nitric acid and mercury, which could be used to silver over penny pieces with a view to passing them off as half-crowns. William's description followed him to Melbourne, where he was soon found although he denied identification, telling the arresting officer that he was Augustus Ryan. In court, he said that he had given the name William Augustus, which was his real name.[92] Confronted by his landlady, who said that she knew him as William Doolan, he had blamed it all on 'the doings of that [expletive deleted] brother of mine'. At their trial, Thomas said that the coin in question must have been passed to him, and that the chemicals had been left with him by a young man 'who went to the country'. The judge described the evidence of manufacturing as slight and on this, the more serious count, the jury found the brothers not guilty. Of uttering, however, they were found guilty and both were sentenced to nine months' hard labour in Sandhurst gaol.[93]

When Thomas was released, in May 1876, he found a job as a stoker on the locomotive engine *Phoenix*, which was then laying ballast on the Sandhurst and Inglewood railway. One of his duties was to oil the tender boxes when they got hot, which entailed standing on the side step while the train was in motion. As the engine slowly approached Derby platform on 25 August the driver sounded the whistle as a warning. Soon afterwards a man riding on one of the ballast trucks behind the engine saw that someone, facing rearwards, had been struck by the first platform post. The driver immediately reversed the engine and called for Thomas to apply the brake but Thomas was not there. It was he who had fallen, and then

> … by some unaccountable means, he was carried about fifteen feet further along the line, at which point he dropped, face upwards, with his head and one shoulder across the rail. It would seem that, on becoming aware of his perilous position, poor Dowling must have let go of the handrail of the tender, for, of the seven trucks behind the engine, three went safely by him before he fell, but the remaining two [*sic*] went over his head and breast, mutilating him horribly. The train was brought to a standstill very sharply, but, on the unfortunate fellow being picked up, he was, of course, quite dead.[94]

There was confusion as to whose responsibility it was to conduct the inquest and the delay, during which the mangled body was kept in a shed, enabled Ann Dooling to attend from Melbourne. She accompanied her son's body from Derby to its resting place in Bendigo, so grief-stricken that she had to be restrained from throwing herself from the train.[95]

Things were not going well for Ann in Melbourne either, although having lost Thomas she at least had the consolation of regaining James, whose time in reformatory was up. William senior had continued the ill-treatment referred to in the Brannock case and by 1877 the Doolings had separated, Ann taking refuge in the house of William junior and Catherine. Her husband had occasionally tried to take her away and, being prevented, usually created a disturbance. He waited for an opportunity when his son was absent to try again but was again rebuffed by Ann. In petty revenge he poured sulphuric acid on a book of Catherine's and some clothing of William's. He was ordered by the local bench to keep the peace for six months on pain of forfeiting a surety of £10.[96]

Such was the state of his family when Jack was released from Pentridge. He seems to have dissociated himself from his family as well as his past. In 1885 he married Amelia Kate Watkins, the daughter of a storeman. The witnesses were of her family, not his, and the ceremony was conducted by a Baptist minister in Fitzroy.[97] If her family knew his history (and his religion) they were prepared to overlook it because the new son-in-law had a respectable occupation. He had transformed himself into a tobacconist and hairdresser, and the couple would live above his shop on the north side of Burwood Road, Hawthorn, between Auburn and Montrose streets. Domestic bliss should have been complete when Amelia presented him with a daughter, Amelia Nellie Florence, in June 1887 but by then Jack was gravely ill. Two months earlier he had been diagnosed with pulmonary phthisis (tuberculosis). It should not be thought of as a romantically wasting disease; more commonly its progress was described as coughing up one's lungs and when Jack succumbed, on 21 June 1887, the doctor listed exhaustion among the causes. At least he was spared the knowledge that his only child would soon follow him. She died in November, and they were interred together in his wife's family plot in the Melbourne General Cemetery.[98] Amelia Kate continued to run the business for another two years but only as a tobacco shop. As in Bendigo, it was Jack who had done the cutting. She subsequently remarried, bore William Follett two children and lived until 1935.

One might have hoped that Jack's redemption and death would have expiated the sins of the House of Dowling but it was not to be. The one other positive development, the marriage of James and his decision to take his family interstate while establishing himself as a cordial maker, was good for him but also served to weaken the Melbourne family circle. Even before Jack died his father and mother had reopened hostilities. By the beginning of 1886 the two were again living together but violence had resumed. Annie, their youngest child, had also been assaulted by her father and turned out of the house. William's defence, on being charged with the assault, was that he had disapproved of Annie leaving home to live in the house of Richard Walton, a married man separated from his wife and living with another woman. Annie had not been paying rent. William said that he had cautioned her at the time and when she returned had told her to leave. He denied the assault and that he wanted to turn her out but the Hotham bench was unconvinced. It fined him, with costs, and directed that the proceeds be given to Annie that she might pay for board and lodging, but strongly advised her to leave Walton's and 'go to a situation'.[99]

Implicit in William's defence and the bench's advice was concern for Annie's reputation. She was then about twenty and described by a court roundsman as 'in delicate health respectably dressed'. It clearly elicited sympathy, which might have been withheld had the court known that in Fitzroy a year earlier she had been arrested 'drunk and disorderly', the latter usually a euphemism for soliciting.[100] And she ignored the advice, as we shall see.

Her elder sister Catherine was also in trouble. In 1887 she

had been charged with bursting into the house of cab driver Peter Fullerton 'using most disgusting language and threatening to do for him'. Fullerton claimed that her husband Albert Murray, also a cabman, was a drunkard and that she was 'rather partial to the bottle herself'. Catherine blamed the conduct of Fullerton's children. The bench bound her to keep the peace for three months and tut-tutted that 'bad language in a woman was a horrible thing'. Catherine was not in fact married to Murray although she had borne him a short-lived child in 1883.

Like Annie, Catherine seems to have been drawn like into Richard Walton's orbit. Both lived at separate times under his roof, which leads one to suspect that his was a bawdy house. We get a glimpse of the complex relationships involved when in 1888 Annie was charged with the attempted murder of Louisa Scott. Scott was the 'other woman' referred to in Annie's earlier case against her father and Annie was jealous of Scott's 'housekeeping' arrangement with Walton. On 14 February Annie knocked on the door of Walton's house in Leeds Street, Footscray, and asked to see Mrs Martin. This was Catherine, who claimed to be the widow of a man of that name who had died in 1877. There is no record of such a marriage. Scott told Annie that Mrs Martin was not in, whereupon Annie had called her a liar, drawn a revolver and fired at her, the bullet lodging in the door jamb. Annie then ran away to her father's house, where she was living in spite of all that had gone before, but on being brought back to Walton's by the police for identification took the opportunity to punch Walton in the mouth. The gun could not be found although William Dowling testified that his daughter had been in possession of one belonging to her brother James.

Annie's counsel asserted that it was Scott who had been jealous, describing Scott and Walton as 'a bad lot', and that the whole affair had been a frame-up. In the absence of the weapon the bench declined to commit Annie for trial and she was discharged. Two weeks later and re-armed, this time with pepper, she tried to throw it into Scott's face and said that she 'would do for her this (or next) time'. She then threw pepper at Walton outside Donnelly's hotel and followed it up with a barrage of stones. Scott asked only that Annie be bound over to keep the peace but when the latter 'muttered something about leaving the district and going to live with her brother at Fitzroy' the bench suggested that she do so without delay.[101]

Although sister Catherine was only in her late 30s, she was by now a physical wreck. Alcoholism had atrophied her brain and she was suffering from chronic kidney disease. She was admitted to Melbourne hospital and died there on 10 October 1890. The death certificate stated that her rank was that of lady, presumably by virtue of marriage to Murray who claimed to be the son of a gentleman. By then the assertion of marriage was true: with her deterioration probably obvious, Murray had made an honest woman of her four months earlier.

One year less a day, in the same hospital, her mother Ann succumbed to pneumonia. It is unclear whether she and William were still together but it seems doubtful given that as recently as December 1889 William Augustus, his mother's protector, had assaulted William senior in Footscray. The police described the son as 'well known' in North Melbourne as the former keeper of an oyster shop, but whether notoriously or respectably they did not say.[102] And again, that was not the only time William

Augustus was wanted for the offence: there was a warrant out for him in 1892 for an assault on one Thomas Cochrane, and Constable Mackay got a dose of the same when he tried to execute it.[103]

William senior had become a night watchman for the Melbourne Harbour Trust and in his later years lived near Williamstown where, after Ann's death, the family survivors gathered, west of the Yarra. James came to the area and William Augustus and Annie also gravitated there. And it was James who in 1894 reported that his older brother had died in Spotswood. William Augustus had suffered a diabetic collapse at the age of 42. He was buried in a plot that already held his mother and his sister Catherine in the Roman Catholic section of Melbourne General Cemetery.

William senior was the next to go, in 1897. Annie must have forgiven him because it was her de facto husband William Richardson who informed the registrar that his father-in-law had died at the Richardsons' house in Hope Street, Spotswood. William senior was buried in the Williamstown cemetery, whence James followed him in 1915. As with Jack, tuberculosis was James's nemesis. Three months of oxygen starvation ended in asphyxiation. He was not quite the Last of the Doolans; that was Annie, who emphatically outlived all her siblings. She died, full of years and survived by a flock of descendants, at Footscray in 1950.

It is a remarkable family history. All of the Dowling children had survived infancy but two had been killed in accidents and two others had fallen victim to disease before either of their parents died. All had had brushes with the law. Only the youngest, Annie, lived beyond the age of 51. A strange fatality.

Afterword

In 1882 Jack Doolan vanished into the anonymity of Australia's largest city. By then, the *Wild Colonial Boy* had already moved on. If the theatre circuit was, as suggested, its conduit, then the Bendigo and Castlemaine 'hits' would in time have lost their relevance. The further and longer it roamed from its birthplace the less recognizable as satire the song would have become. By the time it resurfaced in Mansfield it was probably already carrying Harry Power's Beechworth baggage. It certainly was by 1881, when no hint of satire remained and Hodgson played it straight, not suspecting that John Dooling, a child who had left Castlemaine by the age of three, might be Jack Dowling, bushranger. By the time Paterson collected the song, a quarter of a century later, it had acquired Bold Jack Donohue's chorus and was a fully-fledged folk song.

The two main forces at play in the song's transformation from satire to folk ballad would have been idealization and standardization. To the classes from whose ranks they largely came the bushrangers were heroes, not objects of condemnation, ridicule or pity. The element of ridicule would have been lost from *Wild Colonial Boy* because people wanted to believe that its satirical inversions and exaggerations were statements of fact. Standardization would have followed as attempts were made to have Jack conform to the conventions of bushranger behaviour.

• Jack should have robbed the rich to help the poor (or at least to have refrained, as Harry Power sometimes did, from robbing the poor or helpless). In the Hodgson version Jack simply takes Judge Macoboy's gold, no beg pardons. In the Paterson version, it is implied that the gold is taken because the judge hasn't 'acted on the square', robbing a mother of her son and only joy. Although both versions of this incident may be of equal antiquity, singers have preferred Paterson's; Jack now only robs those who deserve to be robbed.

• Bushrangers were required to be dismissive of authority, as Power and Ned Kelly were. In Walter Cooper's play *Colonial Experience* (1868), a character quotes what is alleged to be a colonial proverb: 'I'm free and you're my equal, as the bushranger said ven he stuck up the judge'. Some similarly flash remark has to be attributed to Jack, hence his lecture to Macoboy.

• Jack should have gallantly accepted a fight against odds, like Bold Jack Donohoe and Ned Kelly. In Jack's story there were too many bushrangers and not enough police (traditionally three, as in *Walzing Matilda*'s 'troopers one, two, three'). If Ned Donnelly ever figured in the song this is where he would have to be eliminated, to lengthen the odds against Jack.

• Jack should have resisted, to the end if necessary, 'dying game' like Donohoe. This is where confusion sets in among the standardizers. Some have him die on the spot, others have him suffer a 'mortal' or 'awful' wound. If he has to be captured he must at least wound some of his assailants, as Ned Kelly did (subsequently dying game on the gallows).

By the end of the century the song had emigrated. When

and how it acquired the tune that popularly replaced *Wearing of the Green* remains unclear. The folklorist A. L. Lloyd attributed the 'doleful waltz' to an unnamed stage comedian who attached it to *Wild Colonial Boy* in Ireland, circa 1900.[104] The Oxford Companion to Australian Folklore identifies the comedian as Percy French[105], the composer of Irish classics like *Mountains o' Mourne* and the song beloved of generations of undergraduates, *Abdul Abulbul Amir*. If so, the song had migrated via North America, for in it Jack (now surnamed Duggan[106]) was said to have loved the prairie, where rangers rode along. Intriguingly, in this version Jack stabs McEvoy (Macoboy) in what might be a corrupted reference to the Zahner incident. That the song reappears on a stage is perhaps evidence that it was carried from Australia by the Irish theatrical diaspora. There were many professionally Irish performers, fake as well as real, touring the English-speaking world during the gold rush era. The 'Irish colonial' songs of one of them, Joe Small, a Bendigo favorite, had been published by Arthur Hodgson in his first *Colonial Songster*, c.1857. The Zavistowski Sisters, Polish-Americans who headlined in Harry Stanley's last pantomime at the Lyceum, had left for Sydney and home at about the time that Jack and Ned were being arrested. Who can say what was in their baggage.

In Australia, the Kelly connection guaranteed that *Wild Colonial Boy* would become an anthem of the bush, second in popularity only to *Waltzing Matilda*. The link was reforged when Douglas Stewart had Joe Byrne sing the 'wild and beautiful song' in his 1943 play *Ned Kelly*. By 1970 Ned and the Boy were welded together; Mick Jagger sang the waltz version while portraying Ned in Tony Richardson's Kelly film. The appropriation that the

Royal Commission had suspected in 1881 was becoming a fact, but still the Boy's name was Doolan, not Kelly.

The durability of the Doolan/Boy connection was most severely tested in 1952, when John Ford used the song in *The Quiet Man*. In the film, Ford's homage to his Irish origins, John Wayne plays an American returning to the place of his birth. To provide an excuse for the song, his grandfather is supposed to have died in the penal colony of Australia. Yet the song is not said to be about Sean Thornton, the name of the Wayne character and of his grandfather. Even in the drunken *a capella* version sung by Wayne and Victor McLaglen as they stagger home after the climactic donnybrook, the Boy's name is Jack Duggan. By 1952 strenuous efforts had already been made by Irish folklorists to prove that the song originated in Ireland, and that the Boy's birthplace was Castlemaine in County Kerry. It is hard to say whether their efforts were helped or hindered when in 1950 a Dublin music house claimed copyright over the 'American' lyrics and the waltz tune in the name of Joseph M. Crofts. Appropriation, not imitation, is the sincerest form of flattery. That said, it is to the Irish world-empire that *Wild Colonial Boy* owes its fame. *Waltzing Matilda* is internationally known as an Australian folk song, but *Wild Colonial Boy* is Australia's only international folk song. Jack Doolan has travelled a long way from Castlemaine.

Incurable romantics will insist that the story told here cannot be right. There must be another Jack Doolan, or a boy with a name something like, still waiting to be discovered. If there is, it can be confidently predicted that he will be found not to have robbed the Beechworth mail, nor to have lectured Judge Macoboy, nor to have been shot by Kelly, Davis or Fitzroy. His claims to being the Boy can be no better than our Jack's even if he is another juvenile bushranger, which seems beyond the bounds of possibility. John Manifold, were he still here, would tell us not to waste our time. His big question remains unanswered – who wrote the ballad?

Although it stretches the threads of evidence nearly to breaking point, there is one further possibility that should be canvassed. It is curious that a semi-literate boy like Jack Doolan was more than once punished for offences involving writing materials. Harry Power was there in Pentridge at the same time and so was Ned Kelly, his apprentice in bushranging. Pat Edwards, in the imaginative leap referred to at the beginning of this work, treated the story as a boy's fantasy about being a famous bushranger. Could Jack, or a fellow prisoner, have taken his personal particulars, appropriated Power's exploit, and written a ballad? Unlikely perhaps, but it would at least explain how Castlemaine, known to only a few as Jack's birthplace, came to be mentioned in the song; or at least it would, if we did not know that Jack believed that he had been born in Bendigo. [107] And what would then still have to be explained is how the song escaped from Pentridge and became so widely known, years before Jack got out.

Again we see Ned Kelly, still recovering from his wounds, staring out of the guard's van as the train takes him to his committal in Beechworth. He is softly singing bushranging songs to the rhythm of the rails. Thanks to the Mansfield journalists we can be reasonably confident that he had been familiar with *Wild (or Bold) Colonial Boy* for at least a year and a half. Had he learnt the song in Pentridge, claimed it for his cause, and thereby started it on its road to fame?

KELLY IN THE GUARD'S VAN EN ROUTE TO BEECHWORTH.
"WHEN HE CAME IN SIGHT OF THE STRATHBOGIE RANGES, HE EXCLAIMED, 'THERE THEY ARE; SHALL I EVER BE THERE AGAIN?'"

Ned Kelly on his way to Beechworth. *Australasian Sketcher*, 14 August 1880.
By permission of National Library of Australia

Notes & Sources

Preface

1 Mary Burke (who had claimed to be the widow of a man named Nowlan) was transported on the same ship as her sister Ann, and likewise married a Tasmanian convict, in her case Francis Filbin. Both families resided in Bendigo in the 1860s and were in contact, not always amicably.

Introduction

2 Ron Edwards' *Australian Folk Songs* (fifth edition, Ram's Skull Press, Kuranda, 1994) gives 23 variants of the first line of the song with ten variants of the surname. Dowling is the most common (8 mentions), followed by Doolan (7). Doolin appears twice, once with John as the given name.

3 R. Ward, Felons and Folksongs, *Meanjin*, Melbourne, September 1956.

Sing a Song for Sixpence

4 At a concert at Coimadai on 12 July, where it was performed by a Mr E. Burns. *Bacchus Marsh Express* 20/7/1878.

5 *Police Commission*, Minutes of Evidence taken before Royal Commission on the Police Force of Victoria, Government Printer, Melbourne, 1881, pp. 279–80.

6 Boucicault felt obliged to omit the song from a Dublin production after the Fenian bombing at Clerkenwell in 1867 because of the 'political excitement agitating the country at this moment' (*Freeman's Journal*, Dublin, December 1868). The American edition of the sheet

music (C.W.A. Trumpler, Philadelphia, 1865) dedicated the song to the Fenian Brotherhood. There is a tradition that the song was banned throughout the British Empire but in Australia it appears to have been included whenever the play was produced.

7 Anon., *The Kelly Gang, or The Outlaws of the Wombat Ranges*, published by G. Wilson Hall, Mansfield, 1879, p.109. Hall was one of those who later agitated for an enquiry into police behaviour during the Kelly outbreak and subsequently served on the Royal Commission.

8 *The Colonial Songster*, A.T. Hodgson, Castlemaine, (second series, c.1881), pp. 7–8 & 15.

9 A.B. Paterson, *Old Bush Songs*, E.W. Cole, Melbourne, 1905, pp. xiv–xv.

10 *Argus* 30/3/1950, 6 & 13/5/1950.

11 Related by J.S. Manifold (*Who Wrote the Ballads?* Australasian Book Society, Sydney, 1964, p. 45), who incorrectly described them as Macoboy's daughters. The judge had only one daughter, Alice, who died in 1904.

12 When her father died, in 1904, Mrs Bland was only eleven years old. Her father also had been young – fifteen – when his father the judge died. By the time Mrs Bland wrote to Turnbull even the events of which she had first-hand childhood knowledge were nearly half a century past.

13 J. Meredith, *The Wild Colonial Boy*, reprinted by Red Rooster Press, Ascot Vale, 1982, pp. 42–5.

14 J.S. Manifold, *op. cit.*, pp. 35–47.

15 *Mount Alexander Mail* 15/1/1858.

16 P. Edwards, *The Wild Colonial Boy*, reprinted by Reed Books, French's Forest, 1984, inside back cover.

The Boy Who Stabbed John Zahner

17 Archives Office of Tasmania, Tasmanian Convicts, Studio Q, Hobart, 2000.

18 National Archives of Ireland, Transport Registers TR7 p. 134 and

TR9 p. 82 (F) respectively.

19 Archives Office of Tasmania, Convict Permissions to Marry, 52/5, pp. 101–2. Married 7/6/1852, certificate 1852/0667.

20 Archives Office of Tasmania, Tasmanian Pioneers Index 1803–1899.

21 Registry of Births, Deaths, and Marriages Victoria, Victorian Pioneers Index, 1836–1888.

22 Stevens and Bartholomew's *Sandhurst, Castlemaine etc. District Directory*, 1867.

23 *Bendigo Evening News* 8 & 13/1/1869 and *Bendigo Advertiser* 14/1/1869.

24 *Bendigo Independent* 16/1/1869.

25 *Bendigo Evening News* 19/1/1869, *Bendigo Advertiser* and *Bendigo Independent* 20/1/169.

Reformatory

26 Health and Community Services Victoria (HCSV), Children's Register of State Wards, Old Series (Admissions) 1864–80, vol. 5, folio 24.

27 *Industrial and Reformatory Schools*, Report of the Inspector for the year 1869, Government Printer, Melbourne, 1870.

28 *Bendigo Evening News* 25 & 26/2/1870.

29 HCSV, Children's Register of State Wards, OS vol. 5, folio 193.

30 *Victoria Police Gazette* 7/5/1868 and *Bendigo Advertiser* 14/5/1868.

31 Evidence of G.O. Duncan, Inspector of Industrial Schools, in Report No. 3 of the Royal Commission on Penal and Prison Discipline, Government Printer, Melbourne 1872, p. 6.

32 *Victoria Police Gazette* 29/3/1870.

33 *Victoria Police Gazette* 26/4/1870.

34 *Bendigo Evening News* 25/8/1871.

35 Inquests into fires in Victoria were at the discretion of the local coroner.

36 *Bendigo Independent* 26/8/1871.

Macoboy's Law

37 *Bendigo Evening News* 22/3/1871.

38 B.T. Mansbridge, Judge Macoboy and the Wild Colonial Boy, *Chronicle: Journal of the Clerks of Courts*, vol. 27, nos. 1 & 2, March & June 1987.

39 Report No. 2 of the Royal Commission on Penal and Prison Discipline, Government Printer, Melbourne, 1871, pp. 16–18.

40 Ibid., pp. xii–xiii.

The Sugarplum Kids

41 The events from 16/12/1871 to 9/1/1872 have been reconstructed from newspaper accounts of the boys' arrest and committal, especially the *Bendigo Advertiser* and *Bendigo Independent* of 10/1/1872 and the *Bendigo Evening News* of 16/1/1872.

42 There were hybrids of this description. The French Le Mat had an upper barrel with a revolving cylinder and a lower barrel with a single shotgun round.

43 *Bendigo Advertiser* 10/1/1872.

A Mother's Anguish

44 Macoboy was terminally ill, and the hearings in chambers that day were his last.

45 *Bendigo Advertiser* 17/1/1872. Sons William and Thomas are nowhere mentioned in the newspaper accounts.

46 The evidence given at the committal hearing is mainly as reported in the *Bendigo Evening News* of 16/1/1872.

47 *Bendigo Evening News* 16/1/1872.

48 *Bendigo Independent* 17/1/1872.

49 *Bendigo Evening News* 18/1/1872.

50 *Bendigo Advertiser* 23/2/1872.

51 *Bendigo Evening News* 3/8/1870.

52 Reprinted in the *Mount Alexander Mail* of 22/2/1872.

53 *Bendigo Independent*, reprinted in the *Waranga Chronicle* of 29/2/1872.

54 *Bendigo Advertiser* 26/2/1872.

55 *Bendigo Advertiser* 11/1/1872 and 20/2/1872.

56 Compare it with the five-year sentence Justice Williams handed out a year later to James Kelly, Ned Kelly's 14-year-old brother, for four counts of cattle stealing. (As far as one can tell, Jack Doolan's use of young Kelly's name as an alias is coincidental.)

57 *Bendigo Advertiser* 26/2/1872.

The Makings of a Legend

58 *Bendigo Advertiser* 24/2/1872.

59 *Bendigo Advertiser* 28/2/1872.

60 HCSV, Children's Register, OS vol. 5, folio 410.

61 *Bendigo Advertiser* 29/2/1872.

62 HCSV, Children's Register, OS vol. 5, folio 410. Parentheses in original.

63 *Bendigo Advertiser* 28/2/1872. A 'flogging bill' did come before the Victorian Parliament, but it failed to pass. Shortly thereafter an Act to introduce compulsory education became law.

64 *Argus* 26/12/1865.

65 *Bendigo Evening News* 24/11/1868.

66 *Bendigo Evening News* 29/1/1870.

67 *Bendigo Evening News* 7/7/1870.

68 *Bendigo Evening News* 24/1/1870.

69 *Bendigo Evening News* 22/12/1871.

70 *Mount Alexander Mail* 10/1/1872.

71 *Mount Alexander Mail* 15/1/1872.

72 *Bendigo Advertiser* 19/3/1872.

73 *Bendigo Evening News* 12/2/1869 and *Bendigo Advertiser* 17/1/1872.

74 It is highly likely that the *Independent*'s court reporter in January 1869 was the man who also covered Jack Doolan's court appearances for the *Advertiser* in 1872: John Quick, later one of the fathers of Federation and annotator of the Australian Constitution, was working his way towards a career in the law. In his retirement he began compiling a Book of Australian Authors, but his papers (NLA MS 53) do not mention the Wild Colonial Boy.

Fourteen Years Hard

75 Report No. 2 of the Royal Commission on Prison and Penal Discipline, *op. cit.,* para. 16.6.

76 PROV, Central Prisoner Records Males, VPRS 515/14, No. 9556.

77 Progress Report of the Royal Commission on Prison and Penal Discipline, Government Printer, Melbourne, 1870, Appendix D.

78 Ibid., p. 15.

79 He left A Division at about the time Ned Kelly entered it. Kelly, a year older than Jack, was serving three years for receiving a stolen horse. Harry Power was also in Pentridge at the time.

80 Evidence of Robert Neal, overseer of shoemakers in Pentridge, Progress Report of the Royal Commission, *op. cit.*, p. 21.

81 *Bendigo Advertiser* 3/9/1875.

82 J.S. James, *The Vagabond Papers*, Hyland House, Melbourne, 1983, p. 91.

83 PROV, Central Prisoner Records Males, VPRS 515/14, No. 9557.

84 The cat and the birch were not formally abolished until 1957.

The Ballad of Jack Doolan

85 Henry Lawson, *The Songs They Used to Sing*, in *On the Track*, Angus & Robertson, Sydney, 1900.

An Unfortunate Family

86 Calculated from data in the Return of Offences and Sentences, Penal Establishments and Gaols, Report of the Inspector-General for the year 1882, Government Printer, Melbourne, 1883, p. 7.

87 Memorandum from Penal and Gaols Department to Victorian Discharged Prisoners' Aid Society re James (in place of 'John', crossed out) Doolan, Victorian State Library MS 10663, Box 64.

88 Ned Donnelly similarly defied expectations. After release in 1885 he got a job with the railways, married and had four daughters. When he died in Richmond in 1923 it was as a respectable citizen who had not been in trouble with the law for nearly four decades.

89 *Bendigo Advertiser* 13/9/1872.

90 He was fourteen.

91 *Bendigo Advertiser* 17/9/1873.

92 Most of Doolan children had middle names that were not recorded on their birth certificates. The other surviving children were named, in order of birth, Catherine Anastasia, John George, James Patrick and Annie Agnes.

93 *Bendigo Advertiser* 26 & 31/8/1875, 2 & 18/9/1875.

94 *Bendigo Advertiser* 4/9/1876.

95 *Argus* 26 & 29/8/1876 and *Bendigo Advertiser* 28/8/1876.

96 *Argus* 5/4/1877.

97 Victorian Registry of Births, Deaths and Marriages, Melbourne marriage certificate No. 3073 of 1885. The certificate is the first official documentation to record that Jack had a second given name, George. He says he is the son of William Dowling and Ann, maiden name Bourke. He gives his age as 28, one year out, and says that he was born in Sandhurst which repeats a mistake first made in

his Pentridge record.

98 Southern Metropolitan Cemetery Trust, Melbourne General Cemetery, Other Denominations, Monumental, Compartment G, Grave 101.

99 *North Melbourne Advertiser* 30/4/1886.

100 *Mercury and Weekly Courier* 14/3/1885.

101 *Argus* 16, 21, 27 & 28/2/1888 and *Independent* (Footscray) 25/2 & 3/3/1888.

102 *Victoria Police Gazette* 9/12/1889 & 23/1/1890.

103 *Victoria Police Gazette* 10 & 17/8/1892.

Afterword

104 A.L. Lloyd, sleeve notes to *The Great Australian Legend*, Topic Records, London, 1971.

105 E. Waters in G.B. Davey and G. Seals (eds.), *Oxford Companion to Australian Folklore*, OUP, Melbourne, 1993, p. 164.

106 Dick Duggan was the bushranger in George Darrell's play *The Sunny South* (1883).

107 Unlike his reformatory record, which gives his 'native place' as Castlemaine, Jack's Pentridge documentation says that it was 'Victoria (Sandhurst)'. The discrepancy probably arises from native place being taken in the first instance to mean birthplace, and in the second to mean residence. There is no record of the family's presence in Bendigo (Sandhurst) until the 1860s.